PLATE CCLXII.

'For me, who has spent many a summer on the Princes Islands, this book is a ravishing account of the enchantment of a poet by the landscape, the light and the people of this archipelago. Joachim Sartorius starts in the present without ever losing sight of the mystical legacy of Byzantium, the life of the Greeks in the shadow of Istanbul and the loss of the cosmopolitanism. He kindles in us the wish to buy a ticket at once and set off to the islands.'

Orhan Pamuk

The Princes' Islands

by Joachim Sartorius

Translated by Stephen Brown

Armchair Traveller
at the bookHaus

'Was there ever a journey which did not hide a secret, or a single traveller who has not lied?'

Jean-Didier Urbain
Secrets de voyages, 1998

'Naples has Capri and Ischia; Constantinople has the Princes' Islands. The Neapolitans can be no more proud of those jewels, which adorn their Bay, than are the Greeks from Pera of these charming islands, places of rest and pleasure, fairytale silhouettes rising up out of the water at the entrance to the Sea of Marmara. Just as Capri is almost as famous for the crimes of Tiberius as it is for its natural riches, so the sombre stories of emperors and empresses and all the high officials banished into the monasteries on Proti, Antigoni and Prinkipo ... have turned these radiant islands into one of the most tragic sites in the Old World. No corner of the earth offers a richer crop of stories of lamentable catastrophe and poignant lessons in the vanity of human triumphs.'

Gustave Schlumberger
Les Îles des Princes, 1884

For Karin

'Stamboul, with all its sea-suburbs and sea-lanes'

S ELÇUK WAS A BUM. I first met him at the Galata Bridge, in a tea house on the lower level of the bridge. He spent the summer there, tapping tourists for cash. In the winter he was caretaker of a villa on Büyükada, the largest of the Princes' Islands in the Sea of Marmara, eight nautical miles off İstanbul.

Strung out by the fierce heat, the traffic and my too noisy friend Sezer, I had retreated to this tea house, into its darkest corner, and ordered a *şekersiz çay* – a tea with no sugar. He was sat on a box by the way in and attracted my attention immediately. How could someone look so tattered and elegant at the same time? Selçuk managed it. He was tall, lean, around fifty years old, I thought to myself, as he approached me and asked – there was nothing awkward about it, as there usually is in such situations – whether he could be of service to me. He belonged to the caste of educated bums. He spoke reason-ably good English and he was the first to make me aware of the poets Orhan Veli Kanık and Oktay Rıfat, for which I am grateful to this day. I ordered him a tea and, at his request, *lokum*, those gelatinous cubes coated in sieved icing sugar, which taste of tired hair lotion. We chatted. I don't really like the lower level of the Galata Bridge. The view is constricted. I miss the seemingly infinite sky over Topkapı, the water, the confluence of the Bosphorus, the Golden Horn and the Sea of Marmara, all the glittering waterways, which invariably fill my head with heat and open space.

I quizzed Selçuk about Büyükada. *Ada* is the Turkish word for 'island', *büyük* means 'big'. The Turks mostly say simply *adalar*, the islands, to refer to the whole archipelago. You can get there in barely an hour from Kabataş, the ferry terminal next to the Dolmabahçe palace. Büyükada, which the Greeks still call Prinkipo, is the largest of the islands.

The ferry from İstanbul stops first at Kınalı Ada (Greek: Proti), then at Burgazada (Antigoni) and Heybeliada (Halki) before it reaches the main island, where it turns around and makes its way back to the metropolis. The rest of the islands are too small, too insignificant, with sparse or no population, or they are private, so that no large public vessel ever calls there.

I knew only the chief island, from a few fleeting visits in my distant past. My first excursion must have been almost twenty years ago. I had taken the antiquated sleeper train from Ankara to İstanbul, which had once been part of the planned line to Baghdad. The sleeping compartments still had brass containers with polished water jugs from the 1920s. They shook horribly, as did the beds and as did I, lying on one. The rails supplied by the Krupp factory way back in the days of the Kaiser were still in service. At Haydarpaşa Station, at seven in the morning, Sezer took delivery of me. She was wearing a light-blue beret and looked like a strangely curvaceous paratrooper.

'Have they shaken you to pieces?' she said. 'Forget İstanbul. Too hot, too noisy. We're taking the first ferry and we're going to Büyükada.'

On the boat she told me that when she was a child she believed that trains transformed their passengers. She had kept her superstition to this day. What if I had not leapt out of the train door, but a tapir, not her friend, but a cargo of cold water? We laughed.

Upon our arrival we took a horse-drawn carriage, because there are no cars on the island, and were driven once right around it. After we had left the town and the villas and a few stately homes behind us, we climbed up into green pinewoods, suffused with the smell of resin. That smell is the first thing I remember now, and later in the valley, I remember the cypresses, pines and plane trees, and another smell, the warm body odour of the sun-baked gardens, streaming into our carriage. That's what I told Selçuk. He said, the islands are sort of a suburb of İstanbul, and yet really are quite, quite different. The landscape, which I had just been describing, is different. The people are different. The life is different. Although not in summer, when hordes of *İstanbullular* arrive and turn the order of the islands on its head.

We left the tea house and climbed up the steps onto the bridge. How suddenly the world shone! Everywhere on the sparkling water were ferries and pilot boats and cutters and mighty red-painted container ships, nosing their way out of the Bosphorus and onto the gleaming Sea of Marmara. Angler after angler sat on the parapet of the bridge, so tightly packed that their lines glinted in the sunlight like the strings of some vast instrument. Selçuk said that he'd like to show me the villa he looked after in the winter, the *konak* of John Paşa, and everything else he knew on the island. It was the end of September. His job as winter caretaker began in the middle of October. He drew me a little map in my notebook. From the ferry building, just keep going right, past the cafés and hotels, then turn into Çankaya Caddesi, 'the most beautiful street in the world'. Continue up it to number 78, which is the villa he guards. We made a plan. One day in late October all I had to do was knock hard enough on the great iron gate of the garden.

That same evening, back in the flat I had rented for myself in Beyoğlu near the Galata Tower, I decided to move to Büyükada. I imagined the Sea of Marmara as a map with all the pale blue lines for the shipping routes, with long and short arrows, with dolphins and compass roses. Who had not passed through here: Greeks, barbarians, the new Romans, Seljuks, Turks, Armenians, the English, Germans, Russians and White Russians? The time of Byzantium was still ticking away, the endless twilight of the Ottoman Empire, then the upheaval of the First World War, such a quantity of emigrants and exiles, a swarm of arrows and references that I could not decipher. I resolved that I would bring order to this swarm. I drank some rakı and my resolve strengthened. One glass later and I thought it was good to know nothing. More exactly: I thought it was a good thing to know so little of the history of the islands. Just a few fragments. That monks had lived on them for well over a millennium and covered them in monasteries. That they were a place of banishment, especially in Byzantine times. Troublesome princes and princesses, disgraced members of the imperial family, advisers and ministers were expelled from Byzantium and stuck in a monk's cell, often for the rest of their lives, if nothing worse happened to them. The putting out of eyes was the most popular punishment. After the Turks captured Constantinople in 1453, a period of calm followed. The Greeks and – later – Armenian families who lived on the islands went largely unmolested under Ottoman rule. In the latter years of the Ottoman Empire wealthy state officials, viziers and ambassadors to the Sublime Porte discovered the Islands to be an ideal place for a summer retreat. Well-to-do families built their summer residences along the coastal roads. Hotels, casinos and parks appeared. The fanciest restaurants and cafés in Pera established branches on Prinkipo, spreading their Levantine atmosphere, up until the middle of the twentieth century, when cosmopolitanism vanished and both İstanbul and the Islands were 'turkified'.

So much else I didn't know. I had the landscape of the Islands in my mind's eye, with its two thousand years of habitation and cultivation. But longevity, long life, is not the same thing as continuity. That evening in my rented room in İstanbul, before I drank my fourth glass of rakı, I said to myself that the Islands would surely suffer from lapses of memory as well, those problems of identity that are so typical of an imperial city. The metropolis, with its changing names – Byzantium, Constantinople, İstanbul – had left its mark on the Islands. The great crises of the Emperor's City, or the Sultan's City, were also little crises of the Islands. But whoever is so full of memories, I said to myself, must also become forgetful. Tomorrow I would go to a bookshop on İstiklal Caddesi, the main artery through the old European quarter, to hunt out a map of the Princes' Islands; there might perhaps be a book or two as well. Little by little I would piece all this information together, these shards and fragments, and my friends would help me. Tomorrow I would first of all call Ferit, my oldest Turkish friend. He had bought a house on Büyükada a couple of years ago; he could give me some advice. The rakı was doing me good. I fell asleep.

At noon the following day, before the ferry went, I met with Ferit.

Ferit is Turkish. To be precise, he's Ottoman. To be absolutely precise, he's Chinese. He radiates calm and he is in the know. As a young man, when his slightly slanted eyes were not yet hooded by swollen lids, he had studied painting in Paris. There he knew the painters Fikret Moualla, Abidin Dino and Arslan. He revered Henri Michaux. In Turkey he had hoarded up the best collection of *karalamalar*. No one else knew what they were, when he was ferreting out and purchasing these sheets of paper, exercises of the master calligraphers, who would write a single letter on a sheet a hundred times, closely packed together, in order to keep their fingers loose. A good *karalama* looks like an early Pollock or a Mark Tobey at his best. Ferit had made his money dealing art: selling paintings, old tiles from İznik and Seljuk pottery of the deepest, most unbelievable blue. But he had never sold a *karalama*. He had written novels, successful ones, and he had set up an advertising agency. From all this he had earned good money, enough to buy an impressive house on Büyükada, built by an Armenian architect in around 1882. Almost every *köşk* and *konak* on the Islands is built of wood. This villa, the Meziki Köşkü, was a curiosity, made of solid sandstone. Which proved useful later, especially when there were earthquakes. We met in Refık, his favourite local, in an alley that ran from İstiklal Caddesi to the Pera Palas, an old hotel designed for the passengers of the Orient Express and whose splendour was beloved of Agatha Christie and Kemal Atatürk alike.

Ferit greeted me warmly. He had for me always something of the authentic old-fashioned Turkish style, an Ottoman perfection of manners, a kind of contemplative and epicurean languor.

'It's the time of the *lüfer*,' he said. 'The bluefish that swim down in great shoals from the Black Sea through the Bosphorus and into our nets.'

He ordered a lavish meal. I quizzed him about the Islands. How the house purchase was.

Why he, given that he already had a house on the Bosphorus, on the Asian side, had to buy another house on the Island.

'An old dream,' he said. 'Perhaps I wanted to copy the writer Sait Faik, who commuted back and forth between Beyoğlu and Burgazada, a neighbouring island to Büyükada, and in the end chose the simpler life, drank tea with small shopkeepers and fishermen and built his stories from a thousand observations of Island life. And perhaps the Asian shore of the Bosphorus has become too hectic for me. I want to work less and stare at the sea more, cook more, drink more, write more.'

His wife had roamed across Büyükada and fallen into a conversation with an old woman sitting in front of a beautiful four-storey stone house. More by chance than design. The woman was proud of the house and showed it to this stranger, except for the third floor. They continued to meet. One day the woman said that she wanted to sell the house. And her daughters, who lived in France, were in agreement.

'As soon as I looked at the house, I was thrilled. The ceilings and walls were painted with fine frescoes in still vivid colours; there were bathrooms of grey marble and a boldly sweeping staircase. All of it original from 1882.'

Negotiating the sale dragged on and on; the Turkish bureaucracy was at its worst, with endless visits to officials.

'The Ottomans were capable of only two things,' said Ferit. 'Waging war and meticulous administration. Anyway, in the end, we had the house.'

'And what was going on with the third floor?' I asked.

'It was a museum. Time had been brought to a standstill forty years ago. In every room the furniture, the fabric, the curtains were covered with dust. Filth from seagulls too, which had got in through a broken window. There was the most exquisite silk underwear from the 1930s in the wardrobes and a ball gown, which my daughter still wears for special occasions. We didn't find out the story behind it until later. The father of the owner, of the woman who sold us the *konak*, had married a very young woman, seventeen years old. She became pregnant. During the birth the Island's doctor had concluded that due to complications only one of the two, the woman or the child, could survive. The father had chosen the child and the woman died. It had been her floor of the house. He had sealed it. A mausoleum, which we now had to open up and clean out. There are unhappy houses,' said Ferit. 'The life of this house was an unhappy one. I can never feel truly at ease there, in spite of all my happy anticipation, in spite of the splendour of the house. We've lived there four years. Amelie, my wife, sorted out the garden and laid out three terraces. She ended up feeding almost thirty cats, all of which she'd had sterilised by the vet.'

Ferit made a gesture as if to say this was women's nonsense. The house was now back on the market. But he longed for the Island, for the view from the balcony of jacaranda trees, seagulls and the sea.

I said goodbye to Ferit, found a book about Büyükada by Jak Deleon and a map of the archipelago in a bookshop, fetched my suitcase and took a taxi to Kabataş, the terminal for the ferries to the Islands. Grey pigeons and white seagulls sat on the black railings. Grey and white on rows of black, like flourishes, calligraphic signals. So much in İstanbul turns into ornament. Pigeons are really mosque birds here.

They patter about the courtyards of the mosques, cooing in droves. People say that feeding them is an act of piety. But I had nothing on me, no sesame rings, no biscuits. The pigeons were restless. They flew off and let a gust of wind carry them aloft, to spin around themselves in the emptiness. Their maelstrom is a symbol for the maelstrom of the city. The calm of the decoration, the soothing contrast between the broad arch and the narrow minaret fights in vain against this maelstrom, against the clamour and clatter, against the honking of Murat cars, the horns of pilot ships, the jolting of yellow melons, against the calls of the muezzin and the bleating of radios, the voices of singers swallowed up in the loudspeakers, which are always turned up too high. I am now exchanging this racket, this maelstrom, I said to myself, for the green calm of the Island.

In the end I sit myself down on a bench on the upper deck, the ferry casts off and glides past the hills of Topkapı. Hagia Sophia is the most stunning sight. She has been everything, hasn't she? Byzantine church, Ottoman mosque, great caravanserai of God (in the words of Lamartine) and now a Turkish state-run museum. I have at home a book of letters by Ernst Curtius, written from Stamboul in August 1871. I like one passage in particular:

'... we rode up into the hills, to a magnificent vantage point, from which one looks out over Stamboul with all its sea-suburbs and sea-lanes.'

It felt like that from the upper deck of the ferry too: in the golden haze of midday, the mouth of the Bosphorus, Topkapı on the right, on the left Leander's tower, Üsküdar and the Asian coast, to my right again, dozens and dozens of ships on the sparkling expanse of water, unloading their cargo or waiting at the entrance to the Bosphorus, and finally, directly ahead, the gentle silhouette of the Princes' Islands. Here is Ernst Curtius again, in another letter:

'We travelled to the Sea of Marmara in order to acquaint ourselves with the Princes' Islands, a small archipelago off the Asian coast. These islands are, as it were, suburbs of Constantinople and appear to be filled with graceful villas, whose terraces rise up out of the sea. The inhabitants are all Greek. We spent the night in a residential house whose garden ran right down to the sea.'

That was in 1871. And today, nearly one hundred and fifty years later? I look at the passengers around me. Are there any Greeks among them? Now in autumn the benches are only half full. Scarcely any foreigners, any tourists. They seem to be almost all natives. A few laughing young men, chewing on sunflower seeds and chick-peas. Older women wearing headscarves, as well as a couple of young Turkish women in jeans and tight-fitting pullovers. Next to me a girl with bad skin and unnaturally long black eyelashes, which lay them-selves out on her skin each time she shoves a sweet into her mouth and closes her eyes with pleasure. On the water, fishing boats with small birds bobbing in their wake. A man selling tea buzzes around between the rows of seating with a tray full of those tulip-shaped glasses on ugly plastic coasters. The boat stops at Kınalıada.

I browse through my freshly purchased book by Jak Deleon, which I bought primarily for its plentiful reproductions of old post-cards and photographs. These reproductions, though of poor quality, shed light on Island life in the 1920s and 1930s. Every steamboat serving the Islands in that period is pictured. You can feel the pride of the photographers. The ferries, named *Neveser*, *İstimbot*, *Aydın* and *İhsan*, were smart vessels each with a slightly tilted, thick, black funnel and a huge paddle wheel. The steamboat service between İstanbul and the Islands, I read, was established in 1846, with momentous consequences. Until that time one reached the Islands in *caiques*, large rowing boats with twelve or fourteen oarsmen. The crossing took almost half a day. Suddenly the archipelago had been made local. In addition, at around the same time the Sultan passed a law allowing foreigners to own property on the Islands for the first time. A rapid influx of wealthy Greeks and Jews followed. In a few years the Islands had been developed.

The ferry terminal at Büyükada is oddly busy. Evidently many people who have spent a day here want to get back to İstanbul. I thread my way through the crowd, past the ticket windows and kiosks. The Splendid Hotel, where I have quartered myself, is not far. The hotel's homepage presents an imposing, attractive white box built in 1906 with two large flat-topped domes, vaguely reminiscent of a pretty Levantine version of Art Deco architecture. Only later do I learn that these domes hide two huge water cisterns, a vital necessity in the days before water pipes were laid from the mainland to the Island. The carriage from the pier to the hotel takes only a few minutes. At the top of the steps, inside the entranceway, under a broad fan of glass, a young man is drowsily keeping himself upright. Not exactly a porter. A couple of minutes pass before the man at reception emerges.

'I'd like a large, old room with a sea view.'

'All the rooms are old,' he answers.

It's the end of the season, scarcely any guests left, scarcely any staff. The large lobbies are empty. Everywhere there are ample armchairs, ghastly oil paintings, huge mirrors in overly ornate gold frames and furniture from the 1930s, spotted with age. I like it all very much.

'I'll show you a few rooms,' says the receptionist. 'You can have a free choice, because there are only a few guests left, and we're not expecting any more.'

I choose a corner room on the second floor with small balconies and a beautiful view of the sea and the landing stage. I press my ear against the white wall. An old habit. I have the sense that I can hear the Island's breathing, the mass of rock deep in the roiling Marmara, the machinery of water and electricity in this mighty rectangular timber building. The hotel is four storeys high, gathered around a tall, white, austere inner courtyard with a fountain in the middle. This inner courtyard reminds me of the *riads* of North Africa. Absolutely everything here is white: the buildings, the boats, the ferry terminal, the tables and chairs, the seagulls.

When I was first on the Island, that one day with Sezer, I'd already noticed this hotel and said to myself, sometime I'd like to stay there. Now, twenty years later, I am here in the Splendid Hotel. The fulfilment of a longing has a comfortably exhausting quality. Time passes with a different, slower gait, and it doesn't mean so much any more either, just the future passing into the past. I don't unpack yet and sit myself down on the hotel terrace in front of the entrance with the autumn sun on my back. Noiseless carriages glide past, two cats, seagulls, the sea, the Asian coast opposite, which must once have been untouched and is now completely built up. Bostancı looks like a Korean or Chinese city, dying down to a yellowish glow in the last rays of sun. Then the night comes.

I am still sitting out on the terrace of the Splendid. I know nothing, nothing belongs to me, yet already I am the owner of a heap of stars, of this breeze coming off the sea, of two, three flies, who landed on the plastic table and then trundled off again, of two, three tired waves, which I see down, over there, on the far side of the road, by the quay, in the yellow glow of the street lights.

It's more beautiful than in the movies.

A feast at Prinkipo

IN THE DINING ROOM of the Splendid three large windows over-
look the still slightly hazy morning sea. But who is it for, this
mammoth breakfast buffet, which takes up the entire back wall of
the room? The hotel's three other guests, an old, fat Turk with his
rustling newspaper and a mute couple by the window, seem lost
in the midst of more than twenty laid tables. I serve myself sheep's
cheese, olives, fresh bread. *Ada çay* to go with it. Then I sample the
jams: quince, rose, orange, apricot, plum, strawberry. Some are tastier
than others. Outside the ferries are already circling the sea. I walk
out of the hotel. The Island has the colours of the summer gone by.
On my left the Anadolu Club building rises up from among the fat
palm trees and untamed bougainvillea, snow white and bulky with a
phoney grey slate crest, which reminds me slightly of the roof of the
Louvre. This place, famous for its summer parties, its wild social life,
is dead and barricaded. All the shutters are closed and will remain so
for all my time on the Island. I stop off at a café on my way to the pier.
The *baklava*, strewn with small green pieces of pistachio, looks too
enticing. Two young cats are playing under the tables. Large numbers
of people are coming up now from the pier. The carriages are almost
silent, only a brief tinkling from the harness as they glide past. Later
Selçuk will tell me that in fact the hooves of the carriage-horses are
shod with thick pieces of car tire. Hence the lack of noise. It was
Atatürk himself who decreed the ban on cars, as early as 1928, having
been so delighted by the Islands and their silence on his first visit.

Over the following days I gradually come to realise that the secret
centre of these small island towns, on Burgaz and Heybeliada as well,
is the *iskele*, where the boats come in to land. From there the houses
are strung out along the shore and climb up the hills. Almost all the

cafés and restaurants are in the vicinity of the pier. And the shopping street sets off from here and leads into the little town. I follow it. The bakeries are fragrant; the gaudy colours of the ice cream parlours are startling. Banks, the post office, a carpet shop, a little mosque, a supermarket, a pharmacy follow one after the other. There's a conspicuous number of electrical goods shops, as if demand on an island for light bulbs, plugs, cables and emergency generators is greater than elsewhere. Here in the centre the houses are small and modest, but step into a side street and immediately there are the most magical examples of Art Nouveau style villas with playful little towers and balconies, all growing up out of lush, shady gardens. Not all the houses are occupied. Some appear so ramshackle, so tattered, that they must have been abandoned decades ago. Suddenly I am standing on a gently rising street, Şehbal Sokak, in front of the Vatican summer residence, a pink painted rectangular chocolate box. Angelo Giuseppe Roncalli, later to be Pope John XXIII, was relegated here by his enemies in Rome. I can imagine the unwilling nuncio in these rambling grounds, reciting psalms, followed by small, plump servers, and thinking wistfully of the Quirinal. En route to the 'Carriage station' I walk past a Roman Catholic church, San Pacifico, which is open and spotlessly clean, with statues of the blessed Virgin and a profusion of worthy monks. Who comes here to pray any more? I hire a carriage and say 'Büyük tur, lütfen!' All my friends have told me I must make this 'big round-trip' to get in the mood, and get a feeling for the Island.

For me it's like a renewal of my journey with Sezer some twenty years ago. The Turks call these little carriages *fayton*, a phonetic transcription of the word 'phaeton'. We drive the length of Çankaya Caddesi, past villas and large properties, past number 78, a magnificent building, which must be John Paşa's *köşk*, guarded by Selçuk, and enter the area called Nizam, which comes to an end at the top of the Dil Burnu promontory, beyond which suddenly all is green and rural. Pines in lush meadows offer themselves up to the sheer pleasure of the sun. Grazing horses. Scattered cows. The Island is split into two halves, the small town and then a large green area, paradise. You can never get away from the sea. We reach the southern tip of the Island. The view runs down over the rocks onto the glassy, barely agitated sea and small coves girded with reddish rocks, which remind me of Cyprus or Capri. At the end of the tremendous expanse of water, the horizon stands out against the blurry sky, clear and hard like a knife blade. The *fayton* stops at a vantage point. Between the bushes the grey rock shows through the green meadow. Muted sound of crickets. A lizard with tiny black and white spots on its pale yellow back scatters at our arrival. A woman in a jogging outfit is resting on a large round stone. She addresses me. The usual: where I come from. How I'm finding Büyükada. I ask her about the deserted farm, which I saw in a grove of plane trees on my journey here. It used to belong to Greeks. They gave it up, she says.

'Why?'

'The Turks don't like the Greeks. They always spoke Greek and kept to themselves. Relations got worse and worse. Then the Greeks became afraid and they abandoned the Island in a mad rush.'

Rarely have I heard such a trite explanation of the pressure exerted on the Greeks to emigrate, because they refused to be assimilated. But it makes little sense to argue with her. My Turkish is rudimentary, her English not much better.

On the return journey on the other side of the Island, the *fayton* passes a bay. Tall, long sheds with green roofs stand on the beach in an extensive and at first inexplicable facility. Some horses walk between the buildings on clay-covered alleyways. The driver explains: this is where the horses sleep at night. I'm looking at Büyükada's horse hotel. He laughs. There are around two thousand two hundred horses on the Island, he says, and in winter barely six thousand permanent human inhabitants.

And how many cats are there on the Island? They are everywhere. They linger by the walls of the houses, in doorways, on stools, under tables. They come in every colour in the world save blue and green. Büyükada is not the Island of seagulls, nor the Island of horses. It's the Island of cats. They live peaceably with the dogs, idiosyncratic animals, which I find equally fascinating. Generally one encounters the Island dogs alone, sleeping in the sun, curled up with their heads between their forepaws, always in the dead centre of a square. All the *faytons* steer a respectful curve around them.

I spend the afternoon in the Touring Café on the upper storey of the ferry building. The view of Heybeli and Burgazada from up here is magnificent, and you can watch who's arriving and who's leaving. The building was erected in 1912 in the late Ottoman style. The interior with the ticket windows is hexagonal in shape under a high cupola, with four smaller cupolas on the four corners of the square exterior. One English architect a little over-excitedly compared the layout of this functional building to the Dome of the Rock in Jerusalem. For a brief period in the 1950s this first storey, where I am now sipping a Turkish coffee with a view of Europe and Asia, served as a cinema. But it seems not really to have found favour with the Islanders, who preferred to sit in their gardens, talk to their roses, have friends over, look at the sea.

In the early evening I meet Ataol in the Milto-Restaurant. Ataol Behramoğlu is Professor of Slavic Literature at İstanbul University, organises mammoth conferences on Anna Karenina, translates Chekhov and writes poetry. He has just returned from a poetry festival in Tokyo. We are drinking black red wine and eating fat, black grapes, watching the incoming ferries and refreshing our memories. He wants to present me to some of his friends who live on the Island. They are waiting for us in a tavern, run by Ahmet Fıstık. This man, Ataol tells me, is a celebrity of the Island. Born on Büyükada and an exceptional cook and drinker, a few years ago he published a memoir of his childhood. He interviewed his former teachers and tracked down Greek families who had in the meantime moved to live on Kos or Rhodes or in Athens. The book was a great success. It's already on its fourth printing, says Ataol, and he's written more books since. But he's not giving up his bar, which he calls Prinkipo, in memory of the old days.

As we stumble along the path by the sea, already from a distance we can hear Homeric laughter. Then a sign in bilious green neon letters: 'Prinkipo'. In front of the bar, on the grass, between a pair of mangy palm trees, stands a table with ten people at it. The table is extravagantly oversupplied with *mezeler*, Turkish starters, and bottles of rakı and water. A dozen dogs and cats and one young reddish-brown foal form a circle around the table. Ahmet Fıstık greets me. A good face, sharp-eyed, tough and wise. Thick grey hair combed back. Now that Anthony Quinn has been dead such a long time, he could play the role of Alexis Zorbas dazzlingly in a remake. I'm introduced to one after another.

That's Karayan, the fisherman.

'His daughter,' hisses Ahmet, 'she's called Macide, very attractive, oh-la-la!'

Özmat, a professor of International Relations who looks like

Genghis Khan, knows his way around French literature and quotes Gérard de Nerval by way of greeting. Arif is a sociologist with a fringe of snow-white hair. Then comes Ömer, the carpet dealer. They are all pretty cheerful, floating in rakı, you might say. Next in line is Füsun, a poetess.

'Though only three thin editions,' snorts Ahmet.

Every minute the waiter brings out a new starter, smoked sturgeon, stuffed aubergine, baked sardines, small, spicy grilled *köfte ızgara* and 'The Swooning Imam'. The table overflows: plates of delicacies are piled one on top of another.

Then there is another Professor of Turkish literature, Orhan, who has a *büyük ev*, a large house, on the Island and a *küçük ev*, a small one, in Kadıköy. Last of all is 'The Philosopher', an Armenian, rather good-looking, except a little leathery, as if he's been pickled in rakı. His name is Kirkor. He asks me immediately what qualities make up a poet.

Ahmet Fıstık pre-empts me: 'A sad and misunderstood person.'

Which is naturally a better answer.

'A little crazy,' I say, 'and perhaps too egocentric.'

'That's it exactly,' says Kirkor. 'Every morning I get up, the first thing I do is I go to the mirror and I say to myself: this is me. I look so good! If a man loves himself – and I do love myself – then he is capable of loving others as well,' he adds.

Kirkor's father was the most famous manufacturer of women's shoes in all of Turkey. His company was called Haiko and had branches in Adana, İzmir, Bursa, Ankara, Antalya, Erzurum and of course İstanbul. Twelve years ago, after his father died, Kirkor sold everything and settled down once and for all on Büyükada.

'It's a good life.'

The waiters bombard us again with new bottles of rakı. The riotous laughter is scaring the dogs, who are meek and trusting. Everyone here has chosen the Island.

'Why?' I ask.

'The calm,' says Kirkor.

'Distance from problems,' says Özmat.

'Could this be, on this little patch of land, the last Hellenistic city?' asks Ahmet Fıstık. 'There are still Greek, Armenian, Jewish elements – and naturally the currently dominant Turkish element. In spite of that! Isn't there still a whiff of cosmopolitanism here?'

He looks around the circle. Everyone nods. *Şerefe! Şerefe!* Cheers! And politics?

'No. We don't talk about politics today. We're all Kemalists, more or less. Even if sometimes we do make fun of the father of the Turks, he got rid of the Sultanate, the Caliphate, the fez. For that alone we must be forever grateful. And of course giving women the vote, not a bad thing either. And establishing the trade unions. The best part is that he introduced everything with such brutal violence that it's impossible for anyone to go back. Even for Erdogan and his AKP. But no politics now. Let's have a joke instead. We prefer jokes.'

Ahmet Fıstık tells it, Ataol translates for me.

'A farmer goes to his doctor. "I'd like a new brain. What do you have available?" – "Well, I've got a French brain, 20,000 Lira." – "Uhuh. Anything else?" – "I've got a big American brain." – "How much does that cost?" – "50,000 Lira. And a German one, bargain, 30,000 Lira." – "OK. Is that all?" – 'I have got, wait a moment, a Turkish brain as well." – "How much is that?" – "100,000 Lira." – "What! That's so expensive! How's that then?" – "It's never been used."'

Resounding laughter. Ataol has to catch the last ferry. He's expecting Anna Karenina in İstanbul in the morning. The group slowly disbands.

I say to everyone: '*Görüsürüz!* See you soon!'

I head back to the Splendid via the shopping street. Full moon. A very delicate light. Some shops are still open. The barber in his salon, over the mirror a swashbuckling portrait of Atatürk with his ice-cold Eskimo stare. The electrical shop. Next to the modest mosque a tea house, men only, at green felt-covered tables. Some are playing *tavla*. A dog crosses the road, limping. A family of cats, all with white fur socks. Further down some teenagers are finishing up their ball game. The streetlamps and the lighting from the Touring Café are blazing, as if they're acting in concert. And at every junction the view over the sea to the Asian shore, this mammoth agglomeration, more beautiful at night than by day: a cordon of lights stretching itself out for over twenty kilometres, and suddenly I long for it, for its many yellow, white, and occasional red lights. I'd like to drive along that endless corniche over there, journey to the end of the lights and then keep going to the mouth of the Dardanelles and visit Troy, when tomorrow comes and the dogs with their curled-up tails greet me barking, barking in friendship.

The world's balcony

FROM ONE OF MY TWO BALCONIES at the Splendid Hotel I look out onto our neighbouring island, Heybeliada. *Heybe* is the Turkish word for a saddlebag, and with a little imagination you can liken those two green hills with a valley between them to a double saddlebag, such as they still use in Anatolia, lying on the sea. In ancient times the Island was called Chalkitis or Chalki, from the Greek word for copper. Aristotle mentions the renowned copper mines, the remains of which you can still see in the Island's southern bay.

I have gained my most compelling picture of Heybeli from Orhan Pamuk. His grandmother built a two-storey house there in 1934. People believed in those days that the air on the Islands was much purer than in the big city and would cure asthma and other lung ailments. Just as the wealthy of central Europe used to make pilgrimages to Davos, so the well-heeled families of İstanbul went to the Islands. According to Orhan, he was first there in the summer of 1952, barely a week old. He has spent many of the fifty-six summers of his life on the Princes' Islands, the majority on Heybeli, the rest on Burgaz and Sedef Ada. In a brief, beautiful essay he describes how his family's departure for Heybeli coincided with the beginning of summer. The preparations were time-consuming. As their summer house had no refrigerator back then – in those days a refrigerator was a very expensive western luxury item – the white monster in their house in Nişantaşı, the area of İstanbul where the Pamuk family lived, was defrosted, then the movers came, packed it up, heaved it up onto their shoulders using ropes and thick straps and finally took it to the ferry, along with a dozen suitcases. His brother and he were always extremely excited, churned up by holiday fever. They ran repeatedly up and down the entire length of the boat, they begged their mother for lemonade and sweets, they went down the staircase to the lower deck and chattered with the cook, who was standing guard over the twelve suitcases and the refrigerator.

Today I'm going from Büyük to Heybeliada. It's barely a fifteen-minute journey on the ferry. In my bag I have a map of the Island, on which, when we met in Salzburg last summer, Orhan has marked the things most essential to him with a cross and added brief notes too. I find his grandmother's house straightaway. It stands on the main street, which runs up from the pier through the valley between the two hills. This house was sold after the family fell into poverty and quarrelled viciously. Orhan then rented another house, one street further up, because he liked Heybeli and he could write there undisturbed. A great part of his novel *The Black Book* came into existence there. I pay my respects to his grandmother's house and carry on to the end of the villas and the beginning of the pine woods. The Halki Palace Hotel juts out on the left. It's much older than my Splendid, dating back to the year 1862. Almost all the guests then were rich parents of students at the Greek business college, which today is part of the Turkish naval academy. In 1992, after a fire, the Hotel was rebuilt in the elegant nineteenth-century style. But I still by far prefer the charms of my old, weary Splendid.

Orhan made a second cross on the eastern peak of the Island. This was the 'gathering place of the gipsy horses', and a little further in a westerly direction you reach the most beautiful vantage point on the island, on the edge of a crescent-shaped bay, which forms a natural harbour. Called Çam Limanı, this was in the good old days İstanbullulars' favourite excursion. In the warm summer nights people gathered in the *gazinos* on the beach, dined in the yellow light from Chinese lanterns and listened to music, mostly sultry guitar-plucking. Later courting couples would row around the bay in the moonlight. Of this place of pleasure, the Chinese lanterns and the elegant rowing boats nothing remains, except a dismal kiosk selling cola and rakı and renting out clumpy yellow plastic pedalos. A couple of teenagers are swimming, and further out, in the middle of the bay, three white yachts sit at anchor.

Orhan made one last cross, on the small mountain in the west,

Ümit Tepesi. On its summit stands Hagia Triada, monastery of the Holy Trinity. From the harbour I climb in a horse-drawn carriage up towards the impressive building. It is built around a chapel and lies in gardens full of blooming bougainvillea and tall, mighty palm trees. From 1844 it housed the Patriarchate's theological college, equal in its significance to the one at Athos and a bulwark of Orthodox Christianity, until, in 1971, the Turkish military regime shut it down. The unrest on Cyprus had grown so bad, the junta in Athens had so fomented violence against the Turkish Cypriots, and Archbishop Makarios III had become so much the archenemy of everything Turkish that the powers-that-be in Ankara made a summary judgement and banned them from teaching. The monastery has been a bone of contention between Turkey and Greece ever since – and a recurring topic in the complex negotiations over Turkey's entry into the EU.

Like all the extant monasteries on the Princes' Islands, Hagia Triada traces its history back to a Byzantine foundation. Even more than at the other monasteries, you gain a sense here of the vicissitudes and calamities of history. The monastery is first mentioned in documents from around the year 820, when Theodora, the widow of Emperor Leo V, was exiled here with her daughters. Photius I, later to be Patriarch of Byzantium, was also stuck in a monk's cell here, for the last time between 887 and 890. He was later canonised and named the patron saint of the theological college. The monastery was completely destroyed at the time of the Turkish conquest of 1453 and then rebuilt a mere century later by Metrophanes III. This Patriarch gave the monastery around three hundred manuscripts, which rank among the most precious from the ancient world and which became the core holdings of one of the most famous libraries in the world. John Covel, a British clergyman, visited the monastery on 25 February 1677 and told of works by Homer, the *Argonautica* by Apollonius of Rhodes, plays by Euripides and an exceptionally early copy of the *Orationes* of Demosthenes. To this day the six large wood-panelled rooms of the library breathe an air of great scholarship, with their bibliophiles' rarities on the first storey of the main building. But the atmosphere is depressing too, because no one makes use of these treasures. There are the metropolitan, a deacon and two monks. That is all.

One monk, who introduces himself as Dorotheos, shows me

around. It's a complete miracle, he says, that this library has survived all its hardships. In 1821, at the beginning of the Greek War of Independence, the monastery was once again severely damaged. Restoration work began in 1844, at the same time as the building of the college, which was for more than one hundred and twenty years the elite centre for training priests for the Orthodox community in Constantinople, and the rest of the empire.

Why do you say Constantinople and not İstanbul, I ask.

'We still use the old words. You must know that the Patriarchate in "İstanbul" has been the seat of the spiritual leader of the entire Orthodox world since Byzantine times. It appoints its representatives, such as the Metropolitan in Ephesus or the Metropolitan here on Halki.'

By now Dorotheos has led me into the classrooms, which are immaculately clean, as if lessons could resume tomorrow. In 2008, his words sound completely anachronistic to me. He continues unwaveringly with his story: 'Then in 1894 an earthquake destroyed all the buildings. Two years later, with the help of Greek philanthropists, the monastery was reconsecrated. For many years, all was well. Even when the pogroms against the Greeks happened in 1955 and many Greek families left the island, the monastery and the college were left in peace. Until 1971. In this year the Turkish government closed down the college. All private institutions in Turkey had to be put under government supervision. The Patriarch protested. You know perhaps that under the Treaty of Lausanne of 1923 the Christian minority were granted the right to their own college.'

'No. I don't know much about it.'

'The Treaty of Lausanne was negotiated after the great fire of Smyrna, present day İzmir. It officially ended the Greco-Turkish war and established that all Greeks had to leave Turkish territory and conversely all Turks had to leave Greece. This provision of the treaty was amongst other things a sad prototype for the many instances of so-called "ethnic cleansing" that were to follow in the last century in many parts of Europe. But there was a significant exception to this ruling: the Greek minority in İstanbul. It was on this basis that our Patriarch protested. But his protest achieved nothing. The Turkish constitutional court decided that according to the Kemalist tradition the state must control all educational institutions. Which, for his part, the Patriarch could not accept. The last students left Halki in 1972. The Turks hung a portrait of Atatürk in the entrance hall, of exactly the same size as the icons. They hoisted the Turkish flag on the roof.'

'And now for many years since, stalemate. How can you bear it?'

'We hope that Ankara will agree to the reopening of the college. Now that Athens has given its consent for the entry negotiations to continue, Ankara has to show, first and foremost, that it wants to belong to Europe and can practice tolerance. The monastery is an important piece of that mosaic. We're expecting positive signals any day now.'

Dorotheos says his farewells.

I walk through the gardens between the main building and the church. The new building from 1894 is a conventional mix of neo-classical and neo-Byzantine styles. But the path leads to a spectacular terrace in front of the church, from where the view lifts my spirit and lends me wings. I am looking out over the world, water and islands and boats and cities and people and Asia and Europe in one mighty panorama. The tranquillity and the vastness tear at my vision. Here is truly the world's balcony. Our souls are small things. They flutter in the splendour of the world. It's as if I'm flying in the light, in the air, in the azure, a cold, glittering blue. It's as if I'm flying from here across the world and as if a world beyond, the true world, is waiting impatiently beyond the gently curving line of the horizon.

Only with difficulty can I pull myself away from such riches, so much light and reflection. The Islands open up a view of shorelines and bays all the way to İstanbul. As I finally abandon the terrace and the spacious gardens, a mild panic seizes me. A gardener opens the gate set flush in the outer wall. These walls, built of stone blocks, served as fortifications. They are the only things that survive from the Byzantine period. As I walk along the walls I find myself thinking about the history and impact of this great empire. The Islands' numberless monasteries allow you to trace out in miniature the lingering death of Byzantium. This empire was once the 'Second Rome'. To the end the Byzantines called themselves *Rhomaioi*, Romans, and placed their emperor in a line that had begun fifteen hundred years earlier with Caesar and Augustus. Today scarcely anyone knows that Constantinople, consecrated in 330 AD under Justinian I, had by the 6th century come to encircle the Mediterranean and by the year 1000 stretched from Italy to the Danube, from Syria to the Crimea. Byzantium was jettisoned from the canon of European history just in time.

Today Byzantium serves at most only as a cipher for decadence, pageantry and imperial hubris. Nothing of the old structures, the forms of power, remains – nothing save the old white-haired Patriarch, who continues to reside on the Golden Horn, continues in the midst of eighty million Muslims to be the leader of Orthodox Christians and uses, as if it were nothing, a nomenclature that has not changed in a thousand years. This continuity has the absurd features of a comical persistence. But it also demonstrates to us that present-day Europe is more than an ancient inheritance of Roman emperors and Latin Christendom, that without Byzantium Europe would have been entirely different.

The path leads me down from the hills toward the coastal road, heading towards the pier. The air grows cooler. A smell of iodine, moss and approaching autumn displaces the smell of horses. On the beach are plentiful mussels, small squares of pale-blue plastic, and shards of glass, worn smooth by the water, milky green, rounded, snug in the hand. From among the mussels, reedy-grey with small white star-shaped pockmarks, I pick up a piece of green glass and warm it in my hand.

The ferry back to Büyükada doesn't leave for another hour, so I visit the cemetery behind the Naval Academy, which dominates the harbour. Among the multitude of Greek graves an old one stands out, the grave of a European ambassador from the 16th century. The stone slab bears a long inscription in error-strewn Latin. Evidently the stonemason's command of Latin was not strong. I labour to decipher it:

> FOR EDWARD BARTON
>
> MOST ILLUSTRIOUS AND SERENE
>
> AMBASSADOR OF THE QUEEN OF THE ENGLISH
>
> A MOST EMINENT MAN
>
> WHO ON HIS RETURN
>
> FROM WAR IN HUNGARY
>
> WHITHER HE HAD SET OUT
>
> WITH THE INVINCIBLE EMPEROR OF THE TURKS
>
> DIED IN HIS THIRTY-FIFTH YEAR
>
> IN THE YEAR OF OUR SALVATION 1597
>
> ON THE FIFTEENTH OF JANUARY
>
> *EDUARDO BARTON*

ILLUSTRISSIMO SERENISSIMO

ANGLORUM REGINAE ORATORI

VIRO PRAESTANTISSIMO

QUI POST REDITUM

A BELLO UNGARICO

QUO CUM INVICTO TURCORUM IMPERATORE

PROFECTUS FUERAT DIEM OBIIT

PIETATIS ERGO

AETATIS ANNO XXXV. SAL. VERO MDXCVII

XVIII KAL. JANUAR.

I'm not sure what should amaze me most: the ceremoniousness, the grand scale of the world of which this young man's death forms a part, or the self-aggrandisement, made vulnerable again by the clumsy writing.

I sit down in a café next to the *iskele* and contemplate the mighty building of the Deniz Lisesi, the Turkish Naval College. Sailors patrol in front of the tall white railings, casting long, black shadows in the late afternoon light. The school can trace its history back to an Ottoman foundation of 1773. After the establishment of the Turkish republic, it became first of all the Academy for Naval Warfare, the Deniz Harb Okulu. All senior Turkish officers trained there. In 1985 it changed into a college for cadets. I remember that I once said to Orhan Pamuk how odd it was that this tiny island (where I had not then yet been) should be a centre for education in war and in religion at the same time. Orhan replied that Heybeli was for him first and foremost the island of happy childhood summers. Those memories cannot be erased. Only later, when the first inflammatory articles against him had appeared in the Turkish press and he had been accused of 'insulting Turkishness', did he notice that many retired officers lived on the Island, fossilised nationalists. Suddenly he felt the Island to be 'hostile ground'. In recent years, though now accompanied by bodyguards, he has continued to show friends his old house. Walking along the seafront, one time when his guards were not being alert, two older gentlemen had jostled him.

'Is your mother Armenian?' they hissed, or worse: 'Did you fuck your Armenian mother?'

He still tries now, as far as possible, to spend every summer writing on the Islands. But generally on Sedefada, the small island just off the coast of Büyükada, which is not served by public transport and is more or less free of day-trippers.

'And Büyükada?' I asked.

'Büyükada always seemed to me to be the wealthier island, in comparison to Heybeli. Once, it must have been the summer of 1958, a glistening yacht came to pick us up and took my parents and me to a party on the beach on Büyükada. I remember the beautiful women in elegantly cut, one-piece swimsuits, lying on the sand on yellow towels and rubbing suntan oil into themselves and the wealthy men, telling each other jokes and boasting about their businesses, and the waiters dressed in white, serving drinks and canapés on silver trays. On Büyükada's shopping street even in those days there were cheese imported from Europe and black-market whiskey. The latest music from London and Paris came out of the bars and you could hear the happy cackling from the Anadolu Club. Back then I thought, this is where the "truly wealthy" spend their time. As a child, from a mixture of shame and envy, I suppose, I was acutely aware of distinctions: between the outboard motors of yachts, between men who after arriving at the *iskele* climbed aboard a *fayton*, and those who went home on foot, between the women who did the shopping and those chic ladies who sauntered around alongside their servants, unburdened by baskets and bags.'

The ferry from Burgazada arrived, white with a yellow chimney and girt with numerous orange lifebelts. A short bright blast of the horn. Orhan had made me attentive to this as well: that every city has a sound that cannot be heard in any other city, an unmistakeable sound. In İstanbul it is the slightly metallic crunching, squealing sound that the *İstanbullulars* have been hearing for many decades whenever a ferry puts in at one of the many landing stages.

The boat is pretty full. Many of the men seem to be returning home from their work in the city, in banks, offices and shops. Most of them are reading newspapers or looking out dreamily onto the darkening sea. In the old days, Orhan writes, the upper-class commuters, be they Christian, Jew or Muslim, used their entrepreneurial instincts to enliven the crossing, organising lotteries and gambling. The prizes were huge pineapples or bottles of whiskey – both of them symbols of luxury, since they were not easily available. He remembered one occasion when his uncle came back home in the evening to their house on Heybeli and held up a large lobster he had won, smiling at its bound pincers.

The ferry puts in at Büyükada. Two young men shove the gangway crashing onto the jetty. I walk past the railings, through the ferry building I have become so fond of, and along the high street to the clock erected on the main square, *Saat Meydan*, in 1923, the year of the founding of the Turkish Republic. Along with the *iskele* and my Splendid Hotel, this is one of the island's landmarks. All the cafés and shops are still open. For the first time I notice a kiosk which offers, alongside magazines and postcards, cut-price syncretism: Madonnas decorated with blue eyes against the Evil Eye; tiny prayer mats with Christian symbols woven into them; painted clay figurines of the Sultana. I especially like the Mihrişah Sultan, with her upstanding bust, Venetian lace, crimson cloak with clumsy gold dots, slippers like roses and peaches. I imagine that all these goods are travellers' souvenirs, brought by sailors from distant lands, and which even the Penelope left at home, full of longing, finds revolting.

I settle myself into the Patisserie Dolci for one last coffee. Their shop window, with its sheer abundance of *baklava*, *helva*, *lokum*, of almonds coated in white and dark chocolate and of crazily decorated multicoloured tarts, compels me each time to linger in ecstasy.

Ahmet Fıstık cycles by and says hello: 'When are you coming to Prinkipo? We're expecting you.'

Ömer, the carpet dealer, wanders past and invites me into his shop. Then a man stops at my table and introduces himself as Ergin, a friend of Sezer's, who once worked for the Turkish division of Sender Freies Berlin in old West Berlin.

'Tomorrow,' I say. 'Tomorrow.'

I'll come tomorrow; I'll call you tomorrow. Tomorrow, I resolve to myself, I will visit the John Paşa Köşkü and see Selçuk again.

John Paşa's villa

'I REALLY LOVE THIS,' says Selçuk. 'Sitting on one coast at night, watching the lights on the other coast.'

We're sitting in the dark on the terrace of 'his' villa and looking past the black outline of Heybeliada, over the deep violet expanse of sea to the lights on the Asian shore.

Selçuk fetches a lantern. I'm nearly used to his face after spending a day together with him. It is the face of a person who has never really been loved, who drinks too much, or used to, who was good-looking once but has nearly lost his looks.

The villa, which he will be guarding for five or six months, was easy to find. It's one of the most splendid buildings on Çankaya Caddesi, which – I confirmed this morning in the exuberance of the early light, the cries of seagulls, the colours – really is one of the most beautiful streets in the world. In a game of late-Ottoman Monopoly I'd stake everything to buy this avenue and bleed the other players dry.

From the Splendid Hotel you walk left past the Anadolu Club and up the street to a large square, in the centre of which lies a sleepy yellow dog, like an Indian cow in miniature, only without the horns.

From there Çankaya Caddesi branches off, running along the coast at about fifty metres above sea level, with many steep side-streets down to the sea, and then becomes Nizam Caddesi, as far as the beginning of the pine woods.

This is where the wealthiest İstanbul families erected their summer villas. The oldest, built between 1870 and 1910, are distinguished by their grand entranceways with balconies resting on white columns and a profusion of Art Nouveau decoration culminating in fantastical turrets on brick-red or slate-grey roofs. Especially splendid and dilapidated is Hacapolu Köşkü, where today the Island's district council, the *Kaymakam*, has its home, in untidy offices under dusty chandeliers. A *fayton* stands by the entrance, the council's official transport and the only 'private' carriage on the entire island, in the sense that it can't be hired. Some metres further along stands the villa of the Ottoman general and writer Ahmet Zeki Paşa, followed by the snow-white palace of İzzet Paşa, chief of the secret police under Sultan Abdülhamid II, then finally a house resembling a Greek temple, which belonged to Sultan Abdülhamid II's son, Prince Mehmet Burhaneddin Efendi, who must have been a kind of Great Gatsby in the terminal phase of the ever more sickly Ottoman Empire. The architrave of this house is richly decorated, with two white and blue painted horses prancing on the tympanum.

These mighty timber buildings all stand in lush, well-tended gardens, shaded by ancient plane trees, palms and rampant bougainvillea. As I amble past them I am reminded of the passage in which Gustave Schlumberger reports his first impressions of Büyükada in the summer of 1884:

'The steamboat puts in at a long pier, perpetually congested with a picturesque crowd. The cafés lining the seafront always have customers. Behind this first level, full of life and movement, innumerable small houses and rich villas climb up the hillside in tiers, laid out in a fan, interspersed with those huge plane trees that one admires so much in the Orient, surrounded by a wealth of trees, climbing plants, flowers, wisteria, jasmine, Judas trees, oleander, in such profusion as one never sees except in the environs of Constantinople ... One climbs up these steep slopes, past elegant railings, flowering hedges and entrance gates, with servants in colourful Croatian or Albanian dress strutting in front of them, past houses with closed shutters, behind which the sounds of a piano or the voices of laughing children reverberate, one walks past gardens, where, among the oleander trees, next to jets of water spurting out of the basins coquettish Levantine women smoke flavoured cigarettes and sip at liqueurs, and the tourist, transplanted here, struggles to conceive that all this sophisticated modern life is unfolding at the extreme edge of the civilised Orient and a few hundred metres further on – beyond the blue tides and this welcoming stretch of coast – the land of unbridled barbarism begins.'

Thus the heady, always rather too metaphor-laden, Gustave Schlumberger, who witnessed the golden age of this archipelago and then with his book *Les Îles des Princes*, scored something close to a bestselling hit in a Paris yearning for the East.

It is now autumn. The white, pink or yellow-painted villas seem like sealed chocolate boxes. The blinds are down, the gardens lonely and empty. Not far from the *köşk* of Zeki Paşa stands the John Paşa Köşkü – Nr. 78, as Selçuk wrote on my notepaper on the Galata Bridge – a long, rectangular two-storey grandiosity built of wood. The ten columns of the colonnade at ground level support a balcony along the entire second storey of the building. The balcony and the façade itself are richly decorated in an elaborate, syrupy French style. Two mini Chinese temples poke out from between the chimneys. This franco-oriental concoction, painted a light beige, was erected, Selçuk tells me later, by Trasivoulos Yannaros, known as John Paşa, director of the first shipping company to connect İstanbul with the Islands. The front garden between the building and the street is slender; the real gardens spread out behind the house towards the sea. Two marble flights of steps connect them to the large verandah on which we are now sitting. In the grounds, near to the wall marking the boundary where the property meets a side-road running down to the sea, stands a wooden shed. This is where Selçuk lives, with a table, a chair, a bed and a huge bunch of keys. When I arrived in the morning, he was fiddling about on the front terrace, so I had no need to knock on the tall wrought-iron gate, as he had recommended. After a welcoming tea, he insisted on giving me a tour of the house.

On the ground floor are the reception rooms, divided up by pairs of golden columns set into the walls. Crystal chandeliers, blinded by dust, hang from the lavishly decorated coffered ceilings. The coffers are embellished with paintings. One room features Egyptian motifs, a camel at a drinking trough, the great gateway at Karnak, the Colossi of Memnon. On the ceiling of another are European motifs, Alps with mountain lakes, fishing scenes, and even Lohengrin on his barque pulled by a swan. Ladies with cornucopias stride over the staircase, very late classical.

'Trasivoulos Paşa was Greek, and he loved pomp,' says Selçuk. 'His wife, an Austrian, loved pomp too. They were well connected. A daughter, by the name of Aliş, married Osman Nizami Paşa, who was the Sultan's ambassador to Berlin in 1911. Evidently the shipping continued to bring in a great deal of money. This house has fifteen bedrooms and reception rooms, three bathrooms, toilets, a kitchen and a huge dining room, on a total floor area of nearly 2,000 square metres.'

I imagine glittering dances, people in their evening dress spinning in pairs under these chandeliers. I ask Selçuk why everything looks so run-down, so frail, and who the current owner is, who plainly couldn't care less.

'John Paşa died in 1918 while taking a cure in Bursa. He was a frequent visitor to the spas there. He was buried in the Greek Orthodox cemetery in Bursa. Shortly after his death, an Italian, Emanuel Karasu, bought the property, and then – in 1936 – came another Greek, Christos Dragonis. I don't know anything about him. Today the house belongs to the grandchildren of Ahmet Borovali, who bought the *köşk* in 1938. These heirs don't really care about the house. They pay me and they come here for two weeks every summer. There are rumours that they have put the house on the market for a couple of million dollars. You'd have to find a buyer who enjoys this peculiar smell of the past.'

The private rooms are on the first floor and on a slightly smaller scale. The splendid medallions on the ceilings recur. The rooms are separated by mahogany doors decorated with inlaid brass. Old photographs hang on one wall in the library. John Paşa as a young entrepreneur, a very alert, serious gaze, the lower half of his face covered by a full black beard. He looks like Johannes Brahms. A cravat holds his immaculate white shirt together; a watch-chain stretches over the beginnings of a paunch.

'And that's Aliş,' says Selçuk, pointing to a photo in an oval frame next to the portrait of John Paşa. She looks likes a classic teenage girl, with a round face, full lips, a small flat summer hat on her head and a string of pearls around her white neck. 'She was a *lâtife gibi*,' says Selçuk.

'A what?'

'It comes from Atatürk's wife. Her name was Lâtife Uşaklıgil. She was very independent and really didn't make life easy for Atatürk. By *lâtife gibi* we mean wives who stamp their heels and run around screaming if their husbands don't want what they want.'

'And that was too much for the father of the Turks?'

'Absolutely. The marriage didn't last long, just two-and-a-half years.'

I look at Ali\$ in the photo and say '*Latif*' – which means pretty and is one of the few Turkish words I know.

We carry on. Lengths of white fabric have been thrown over the furniture and upholstery to protect it from the sun. The floor-length mirrors multiply the pallid gleams of a Palazzo on the brink of disintegration. At the end of the corridor are a few rooms fully supplied with new, pretty dreadful furniture. Here, presumably, is where the current owners camp out in the summer. The last room has the same rich patina, with mattresses piled on top of each other almost to the ceiling.

This house offers up such a wan, blinded spectacle. Yet the pompous and pretentious history of a successful Greek entrepreneur in the latter days of the Ottoman Empire lives on here in an uncommonly intense way. And for me something else lies in the depths of this mirror, something of the life of these families, and a hundred happy, ambitious and acquisitive people, whom I have never seen or known.

As Selçuk leads me through the grounds, past amphorae and cracked statues, copies of Greek sculptures overgrown with grey moss, he says to me in his broken English: 'This place has superior melancholy, yes?'

The paths on which we're walking lead to a fountain with a pump that no longer works.

Selçuk says: the Turks think that there are three sounds that contribute to a man's wellbeing. He says them first of all in Turkish: '*Su sesi, kadın sesi, para sesi.*' – the sound of water, the sound of a woman and the sound of money. He laughs. There is a fountain in the middle of every garden on Büyükada. So that's already one sound there, which will make us happy, he says.

We begin to talk about John Paşa again. At the turn of the 19th into the 20th centuries he was one of the most respected members of the Greek community, which in those days, at the time of the erection of this grandiose building, made up around eighty per cent of the Island's population. There were the Greeks around the landing stage, merchants and craftsmen, the poor Greeks, and then the wealthy Greeks in the summer palaces, like John Paşa. The Jews on the Island were mostly bankers from İstanbul. The Armenians were the fishermen, or they were wealthy merchants and architects.

'And the Turks?' I ask.

The Turks were either state officials, military officers, doctors or else simple manual workers. There was nothing in between.

The gardens do not reach down to the water's edge. From the fountain you can see another building beyond the garden wall, made not of wood but of red bricks. The plaster must have flaked off. It looks pretty ruinous.

'That's Leon Trotsky's house,' says Selçuk. 'The Islands have taken in a lot of people who were seeking refuge, but Trotsky was undoubtedly the most famous exile of them all. He lived in this house, which was built by a wealthy Greek, Konstantinos Iliasko, and which later belonged to İzzet Paşa.

'Trotsky lived here from 1929 to 1933 with his wife, son and two secretaries, who were also his bodyguards. And six Turkish police officers as well. Imagine it! He was bored on the Island. At first he still hoped to be recalled back to Moscow. But as time went by he had to get used to the idea of being a 'man without passport and visa'. When he wasn't writing – either his autobiography or his *History of the Russian Revolution*, in a minimum of four volumes – he went fishing. Some very funny letters from him to Moscow survive, including one to a relative, asking him to send him two hundred metres of strong fishing line for catching big fish.'

Much later I discover a little essay by Trotsky, entitled 'Farewell to Prinkipo', which he wrote shortly after his departure:

'Prinkipo is an island of peace and forgetfulness. The life of the world arrives here after great delays ... It's a good place to work with the pen, especially in autumn and winter, when the islands are almost completely deserted and the woodpeckers appear in the garden. There's no theatre here; there's not even a cinema. Cars are forbidden. Are there many such places on this earth? We have no telephone in our house. The cries of the donkeys calm the nerves. One cannot for one moment forget that Prinkipo is an island, because the sea lies under every window and there is no point on the island without a sea view. We catch fish a mere ten metres distance from the edge of the quay; at fifty metres, we catch lobster. The sea can be as calm as a lake for weeks at a time.'

As I continue my researches into Trotsky the island-dweller, I come across the memoirs of a Turkish author, Mine Urgan, which I quote here without comment. She was a girl at the time when Trotsky lived on Prinkipo. She writes:

'When I was fourteen years old, I wanted to see Trotsky up close. He lived in Nizam, in a house with a garden running down to the sea. No one ever saw him on the streets, but every day he went out to catch fish. One day, when I was swimming in the sea, I saw his boat. It was easy to spot, even from a distance, because he always had his two armed bodyguards with him, one in the front, one in the back of the boat. In the middle a Greek fisherman was at the oars, next to him was Trotsky, who was holding a fishing rod in his hands. I swam up to the boat, grabbed hold of the side and was very close to Trotsky. One of the bodyguards called out 'Git! Git!' [Get lost! Get lost!] but with his Russian accent it sounded like: 'Get! Get!' I pretended that I was exhausted, because I wanted to stay close to Trotsky for a bit. But when the bodyguard lifted up his rifle and looked as if he wanted to smash my fingers with its butt, I pulled my hand away. Plainly they were so terrified of assassination attempts that they viewed even an entirely unarmed girl with suspicion. How wonderful it would have been if that important man hadn't cared about that and had said with a cool glance to his bodyguard: Leave the child alone. Let her into the boat so she can rest for a while.'

I am still standing with Selçuk by the fountain in the garden of John Paşa's house and looking at the reddish structure of the sometime house of Leon Trotsky. He was still living on Büyükada in February 1932 when he was deprived of his Soviet citizenship. How must that have felt to the great revolutionary? Stranded on a foreign island, in a foreign house, looking out over a foreign sea, unwelcome in every European country. Only in 1933 was he allowed to travel to France, then in 1935 to Norway, always a troublesome guest, then finally in 1937 to Mexico. One of his secretaries, a Dutchman called Jean van Heijenoort, was with Trotsky up until the last minutes of his life and later published a book: *From Prinkipo to Coyoacan*.

John Paşa's property and the Trotsky-house are so different.

'Does the Island have an architecture?' I ask Selçuk.

He laughs. He doesn't really know, he says.

Naturally the architecture is eclectic, with elements pinched from everywhere, from Italy, from France. You can find the same glazed fans in the entrances of old hotels in Naples, Vienna or Lisbon as you do over the entrance to the Splendid Hotel. But many of the older houses here have for me something distinctively elegant, exhilarating, the slender balustrades, the delicate pergolas, the airy ornamentation, airy copies of the originals. Now – it is already midday – they rise up out of the many-coloured tangle of plants and blaze in the sun.

Saint George and the Rakı

WE HAVE FINISHED OUR VIEWING of the house and garden and decide to visit the monastery of Saint George. Selçuk bolts the gate, securing it with an antediluvian padlock. Soon the villas are behind us. The grass is lush, a shimmering green, perhaps from the first rains. Horses graze among the pines. Their skin gleams in the sun. I ask Selçuk questions and little by little I learn his life story.

His father was a *kawass* at the British Consulate General in Adana on the south coast of Turkey. A *kawass* was a kind of messenger, who carried out lowly tasks. He had the 'highest' ambitions, says Selçuk, for his six children. Selçuk was the second eldest son. He gained entry to the better kind of secondary school and was always the best at English. The British Consul sponsored him as well. But it was not enough for the University. There was a *numerus clausus* system, administered centrally in Ankara and there was too much nepotism and patronage. His father almost went mad with grief. Selçuk laughs.

'Laughter is the poor's weapon,' he says.

After that he went to İstanbul, where he ended up in a group with artistic leanings, made up of literary types, journalists, musicians, and a couple of people from film.

'I read a great deal in those days,' he says. 'I lived off temporary jobs at printers or newspapers. Then I made the acquaintance of rakı and I got chucked out of every one of them.'

'So there we are,' he finished his story, half bowing towards the sun and the other half inclined at a slant towards the earth. 'And I like this job here in the winter. It's not badly paid and there's hardly anything to do.' He continued: 'I've been doing this for eight winters now. I know plenty of the other caretakers, most of them Albanians. I know the history of many of the houses and, through that, the legends of the Island as well. This monastery of Saint George, which we're about to see, is a place of pilgrimage and bristling with legends. It still plays a major role on Büyükada. Every year on the 25 April thousands of pilgrims come here from many parts of the world – not just Greeks, Turkish Muslims as well and others, not necessarily Christians – to celebrate the feast day of Saint George.'

The coast road we are walking on, which circles round the two mountains on the island in a figure of eight, veers inland, into the broad valley between the two peaks. We reach a junction. The road from the other side of the Island comes here and connects with ours and with the path that runs down from the other monastery, of the Transfiguration, and from this hub up to the monastery of Saint George. This square, formerly known as Lunapark, is portrayed on many old postcards. They show cafés decked with pennants, elegantly dressed ladies under shade-giving pines and gentlemen in their Sunday best on the backs of donkeys. There is still a café today, a restaurant and a round stable, where donkeys still wait to carry tired travellers up the steep path. We go on foot.

The monastery lies just under the summit and offers – like the monastery on Heybeli – a breathtaking view out over the Sea of Marmara, the other islands and the Asian part of İstanbul. Like the other monasteries, it has suffered through wars, fires and the great earthquake of 1894. What we see today has nothing in common with the original church foundation of 963 and almost nothing to do with the new foundation of 1625.

'The story goes,' says Selçuk, 'that a shepherd was grazing his flock here, when he suddenly heard a peal of bells from under the earth. Pilgrims are sold little bells as souvenirs to this day. The shepherd dug a hole at this spot and found an icon of Saint George. That was in 1625, supposedly. Numerous abbots have added to the buildings, so that today there are six modest churches and chapels to see, on three levels. Miracles are attributed to Saint George, especially the healing of the insane.'

Here I must once again quote from my flowery French informant, Gustave Schlumberger.

'Alas!' he sighed when he visited in the early 1880s. 'It has to be said: that a monastery as beautiful as this, in an enviable location, where learned Benedictines have to live and die, passing from study of the great events of the past to the pious contemplation that such natural splendour inspires, that this supremely enchanting monastery should have been transformed not long ago into a lunatic asylum, where vulgar caloyers offer rudimentary care to these poor creatures touched by mental illness ... They say that nowadays the Patriarch also sends to Saint George children and young Christians who are suspected of wanting to become Mohammedans.'

Here Monsieur Schlumberger provides – quite unconsciously, I think – a caustic snapshot of the relationship of deep respect between religions.

In one of the chapels Selçuk shows me iron rings fixed into the wall, where the insane were shackled in the hope that the miracle-working icon of Hagios Georgios Koudonas might cure them. This icon is still to be found in the main church, on the south wall, clad in heavy silver and thoroughly blackened by soot from the candles, clouds of incense and the fingers of pilgrims.

We walk back down the steep, stony path. I can feel every sharp stone through my thin leather soles. Across the valley, on the hill with the town winding its way up it, stands the monastery of Christ's Transfiguration in a thick pine forest and next to it, above the green clouds of trees, a dark wooden structure of huge proportions. Erected by a Frenchman in 1898 in the middle of the Island's Belle Époque, this building was meant to be the most chic hotel on the archipelago, with a Monte Carlo-style casino. But Sultan Abdülhamid II refused it a license and it never became a hotel. A wealthy Greek widow bought the building – reputedly the largest wooden construction in Europe and the second largest in the world – and bequeathed it to the Patriarchate on condition that they would run an orphanage there. 'The Greek Orphanage', as it is called on the old postcards, opened in 1903, until in 1964, as relations between Greece and Turkey became progressively worse, it was shut again. It has been disintegrating ever since, a macabre, comfortless spectacle.

There are now some *faytons* parked on the square where all the Island's roads and paths meet. Tourists are chatting with the donkey drivers. We go into the restaurant and order rakı, water and ice, with smoked aubergine puree and lamb cutlets. Our conversation revolves around the monasteries on the islands and their lost significance. I ask Selçuk if any kind of unity of the cultures and religions here has survived. Selçuk answers that on Büyükada alone there are two Greek Orthodox churches, one Roman Catholic church – San Pacifico –, one Armenian Catholic church, the Hesed Le Avraam synagogue and two mosques. And then three monasteries on top of that, that of Saint George, which we have just visited, the monastery of Saint Nicholas and the monastery of Christ's Transfiguration. Of a fourth, a large convent, where the famous Byzantine Empress Irene was locked up, only a few remains can now be seen.

'I'm not talking about ruins. You're trying to fool me into thinking that Büyükada today is like some kind of thriving Sarajevo. Sarajevo before the war. Does anybody use these churches and synagogues?'

'About twenty-seven thousand Jews live in İstanbul. Some of them still have their summer houses here. And four, five Jews keep the Synagogue in operation. It's heavily guarded. We can walk past it on our way back and talk with the police officers. It's only really open in the summer, but perhaps they'll let us in.'

'And the Greeks?'

'There are maybe two dozen Greeks who live here permanently, but they are old. Many have already died and there are no newcomers. The younger ones have all gone to Athens, Thessaloniki or the Greek islands like Kos or Rhodes.'

The sullen waiter brings us apples and grapes for dessert.

'I don't know what will happen next,' says Selçuk. 'Reportedly there is a small renaissance of the Greeks on Büyükada. Even a couple of Greek-Turkish marriages. But I've seen no sign of it, even though Büyükada in the old days was such a steady draw for Greeks and Sephardi Jews too. Kınalı was always the island of the Armenians, but they have so assimilated themselves – or have been forced to assimilate – that you can hardly tell them apart from the Turks.'

I can't avoid thinking of Kirkor, my pretty, self-loving Armenian, and indeed of all the friends and drinking companions at Ahmet Fıstık's bar. Surely there was a unity on the Island once, which, as so often, politics has destroyed. The first Greeks left the Island in 1923 as part of a population exchange, the next after the pogrom of 1955, then the expulsion of 1964 followed. Which also explains the many houses, abandoned and decaying because their ownership has never been clarified.

'Don't you want to buy a house?' asks Selçuk. He runs his forefinger along the length of his nose and puts on an impish expression. 'You could pull a fast one at the land registry, no question. And there are empty villas that belong to Turks as well. The problem doesn't arise with them. You love İstanbul and you love Büyükada!'

'Perhaps I'll buy Trotsky's villa,' I say. 'I like ruins.'

We toast each other. *Şerefe! Şerefe!* In an instant we're very tipsy, thoroughly inspired by the rakı and by our view from out of the gloom onto the silky blue Sea of Marmara. The sailboats further out shine like ears of wheat in the sun.

'These islands must have been a cradle for poets?' I ask Selçuk. 'Painters?'

'There've been plenty of painters here. I must show you the reproductions in a book that's sitting in John Paşa Köşkü. There's one painter, Ali Avni Çelebi, who lived on Büyükada in the 1920s and 1930s and painted a huge number of pictures. When you look at them, you feel as if you're being touched by the wet nose of a calf. He painted with big brush strokes, he spat on 'purity', for him it was about touch and smell. His seascapes virtually drip; his nudes give off steam. You need a towel or a Kleenex, everything is damp.'

'You should have been an art critic!'

'Hardly! I knew a lot of painters in my time in Beyoğlu and hung around their studios. You'd have to learn something in that situation. But it's a shame that there are no good poems about the Islands. The only truly great Island-writer is Sait Faik. He lived on Burgaz. We can visit his house if you like.'

He paused and studied an imposing, perfect piece of watermelon.

'Orhan Veli is perhaps the greatest Turkish poet of the new era. He swept away all the fustiness of Divan poetry and used simply and precisely the language he overheard on the streets of İstanbul. Artless, yet it was art. Listen to this. The poem is called *Sol Elim*, which means pretty much *My Left Hand*.

> I got drunk and again
> I thought of you,
> My clumsy hand,
> My pitiful hand.

Doesn't that fit us exactly, our situation? In 1941, Orhan published a volume of poetry with his schoolfriends Oktay Rıfat and Melih Cevdet Anday. It was called *Garip*, which means roughly, *Strange*. It was like a signal. These three poets turned Turkish poetry on its head. Today their poems are in all the schoolbooks. I like this haiku from Orhan Veli as well:

> The smell of seaweed
> And a plate of prawns
> In Sandık Burnu.

Isn't that superb? Sandık is a fishing village on the Bosphorus that was known for its bars. Orhan Veli visited it often. Replace Sandık Burnu with the promontory near here – Dil Burnu – and straightaway you have a Princes' Islands haiku. Orhan Veli died far too young, in 1950, just thirty-six years old. And Melih Cevdet Anday, also a wonderful poet, actually moved to Büyükada in his old age and lived here for many years until 2002, when he died aged eighty-seven. But he wrote nothing in the entire last period of his life. It's a shame. A great shame!'

Selçuk looks genuinely sad. The autumn sun falls through the vine leaves; the juice from the melon sparkles on the plates; his eyes are grey.

'He should have written a poem!' He slams his rakı glass down on the table. 'He should've. There are only ludicrous poems about the Island. For example, a song by Çelik Gülersoy, which everyone here warbles. It goes roughly like this: "The large Princes' Island is made up of six beautiful things. First, the blue open sea. Next, the emerald-green pines' – Selçuk makes a sweeping gesture with both arms – 'third, the splendour of the flowers, fourth the lovely houses, fifth the elegant *faytons* and finally the warmth of the inhabitants. And because this paradise is endangered, it must be preserved and guarded." It's a horribly saccharine song, written without imagination.'

He begins to sing the verses in Turkish. It doesn't really sound so bad.

We had planned to walk back into town along the circular road. But we're stumbling over our own feet, so we decide to take one of the *faytons*, which is waiting outside the restaurant, on the square once known as Lunapark.

I very much doubt that the drivers of the *faytons* have any clue about the mythology or the origin of this word. Carriage and pairs like these were first named 'Phaeton' in nineteenth-century Europe, after the son of the Greek sun god, Helios. He had begged his father to be allowed to drive the chariot of the sun for one day. The over-confident Phaeton wanted to get close to the vault of the heavens and lost control of the horses, so that he plummeted to Earth and almost set it ablaze with his fire. For which an enraged Zeus killed him with a lightning bolt.

In İstanbul the *fayton* has given way to the motorcar, though it remained part of the street scenes there into the 1940s. Today it survives only on the Islands, where it is the public transport, something like a cheap taxi. But it still looks exactly as it did in the 19th century. The open deck rests on large thin wheels – the rear wheels larger than the front. Each carriage has two bench seats facing each other in jolly colours with colourful buttons. The canopy is decorated with gaudy fringes. To the left and right of the coachman's block are two antiquated lanterns, which are however almost never lit. The horses wear blinkers. A kind of nappy, generally made of blue plastic, is stretched out under their tails, at the height of the wheels, into which the horses drop their apples. Now, on our way home, our driver stops abruptly, jumps down, takes a shovel from its holder and scoops the horse dung into a waste bin standing by the side of the road. Then we continue. The strapping young man speeds up our horse with his whip. I think to myself, it's as if he wants to play Phaeton, full of too much confidence.

The rakı sloshes back and forth in my brain. The green pines swish past my ears. Light and shade. I look at Selçuk sitting next to me, lost to the world. We are passing the horse-hotel.

'There isn't space for all of them there,' says Selçuk. 'In winter a couple of hundred horses are taken over to their winter quarters on the Asian coast.'

I imagine the scene: a great open boat with a hundred horses as cargo on the wintry Sea of Marmara. A Fellini spectacle. We hurtle onwards. Now we reach the first villas, a kiosk selling fruit and gas cylinders. A golden statue of Atatürk on a small square. Mallukgazi Caddesi. The pink painted Meziki Köşkü slips past my befuddled face. Zağnos Paşa Caddesi. Mighty, old, weather-beaten timber buildings. Then everything draws in closer, and we are in the centre and have left the centre again, until the steaming carriage and pair comes to a stop in front of the Splendid. I pay Phaeton and say goodbye to Selçuk. We agree that we will go on an outing to Burgazada in the coming days.

Room with ferryboats

THE DAYS PASS. In the morning I go out onto my little balcony and watch a ferry, sometimes two or three. I enjoy watching the ferries. I've become fond of these *vapurs*. They move across the water slowly, quietly and gracefully and they preserve so many of the sounds, aromas and traditions of a bygone age. They are a symbol of İstanbul, like the Hagia Sophia, like Topkapı or Rumeli Hisarı. After breakfast – olives, white cheese, honey, rose marmalade – I walk into the village. The displays at the bakery and the *tarteli*, the patisserie, invariably send me into fresh raptures. I gossip with the carpet dealer. He tells me that his father moved to Büyükada in 1952 and opened a greengrocer's. An Armenian friend advised him to open up a shop for carpets and *kilimler* instead, 'because there isn't anything like it on the island'. His father acted on the advice in 1959 and to this day his shop is the only carpet shop on Büyükada. Next year he will celebrate its fiftieth anniversary.

'Perhaps at the Splendid, in the courtyard, with candlelight and belly-dancing,' he grins. 'For my best customers.'

I stroll onwards. I arrive at the fish stand.

'Have you ever seen a bluefish like this one? Look at this turbot, sir! Look at this barbel! Actually, before you do that, look at this sardine!'

At the end of the shopping street the crazy white villas begin and I am happy. I look at the dilapidated Art Nouveau houses, I play with the thought of buying one, the most beautiful, most outlandish one and for a little while I am unhappy. I climb into a *fayton* and have it take me to the *lokantası* on the promontory, Dil Burnu. At this noon hour the restaurant has absorbed the sea into itself. The sea's every broken ray of light is focused on my table. I drink white wine, a dry Kavaklıdere, I toast Orhan Veli and eat *köfte* and bite into a

virulently green too hot pepper. For dessert I treat myself to an anti-
dote, a thick, fat, sweet *kadayıf*, oozing egg white. Turkish families
are sitting in their local, father, mother, uncle, aunt, children. They
remind me of the artless frescoes in any of the Island's numberless
neo-Byzantine churches or in the chapel of Saint George.

I return to my hotel and write. I write in front of the window, next
to the dressing table, with its mirror cracked in one corner. I peel an
orange, I eat the segments, I write. In the evening the seagulls return
to the landing stage in bright flocks. Two cormorants on the rock at
the end of the coast road watch the sunset, as melancholy as poets.
A heron, commanding and proud, flies over my balcony towards the
interior of the Island. I write and grow tired. I walk to Ahmet Fıstık's
tavern and I warm myself up.

Tonight the sky is too dark for me, the stars too numerous, the
cold too damp. The friends have abandoned the front yard and are
making a racket in the bar. I miss the dogs. I've made friends with
Dima, an emaciated yellow bitch with pointed Egyptian ears. She
comes in. I squeeze and squeeze her neck. The foal is outside and
is straining towards the sounds of the cooking, the pot on the fire,
tugging at the arid branches of a Judas tree. I close my eyes. I am
happy.

Sait Faik's Island

TODAY WE WANT TO VISIT BURGAZADA. Selçuk picks me up at the hotel. He's wearing a scuffed, light-brown suit, elegantly tailored. His eyes are bright. We stroll down to the landing stage. The wind carries the sharp tang of the 'horse station'. The sea is frothy. Everything this morning is easy and transparent and in motion. The cafés are already open, no customers yet. The bookshop right next to the pier has a display of wind-ruffled, sun-faded paperbacks on its racks. It looks like a shop that sells Time. The ferry arrives, sounds its horn, belches out a little black smoke. Passengers disembark, are greeted, disperse. Then the gate is opened and we board.

A *vapur* is the best place for watching people. On the hard benches on the upper deck there are: a pair of fashionably dressed upper-class women, salesmen who have brought vegetables or rakı or lamps to the shopkeepers on the islands, young men in white uniforms, travelling to the Naval Academy on Heybeli, schoolchildren, tourists being pestered with offers of tea from the *garsons* in their crumpled red jackets with black lapels: '*Çay? Çay?* Tea? Tea?' Most of the passengers, however, are as quiet and without visible haste as the ferry itself. It's as if they feel that the relative calm on a *vapur* offers them the transition they need from the Islands to the big city or conversely from the metropolis to village life.

In Turkey there is scarcely any public place where food is not sold, and a ferry is no exception to the rule. The *garsons* offer not just tea, but also biscuits, sandwiches and nuts. And there are young men snaking their way between the rows of benches hawking their *simitçi*, crispy dark-brown sesame-bread rings, or sweets dripping with honey, which wobble threateningly on the round trays on their heads, each time the seller leans forward to give back some change. Selçuk buys himself a sesame ring.

'My breakfast,' he says.

I'm full of excitement. Even the residents of Büyükada say, in a brief surge of magnanimity, that Burgaz is the most beautiful of the Princes' Islands. So why do they stay on their island?

'Because it offers the most amusements,' suggests Selçuk.

Though there's not so much of that to experience in autumn.

The journey to Burgaz lasts something over twenty minutes, with a stop at Heybeli. Burgaz is the third largest of the Princes' Islands. The British cleric John Covel I referred to before wrote in his diary for 2 April 1677:

'We sailed this afternoon from Pera to Antigono, where we took lodgings in a humble tavern. The town has nothing worth remarking. The wine is ordinary, the water of a very poor quality, the bread expensive and not tasty.'

For me however the little harbour makes a very friendly impression as we arrive into it. Directly behind the pier a mighty white wooden building rises up, with four thick Doric columns reaching up to the second storey. The erstwhile Burgaz Palas Hotel, built in 1926, is no longer. The white paint is peeling, the boat engines make the columns shudder, the windows see nothing. There is still a café on the ground floor, with a couple of tables outside in the sun. Four Turkish matrons are sitting at one of the tables. Stout, fiercely made up, with dyed blonde hair, which is growing back, it seems, a merciless jet-black, they chatter and smoke competitively.

Selçuk and I walk the hundred metres uphill to the main square, which is dominated by a large, brawny-looking church. Its dome floats on a wreath of pale-green pine treetops.

'It's late nineteenth-century,' says Selçuk, who's noticed my disappointment. 'But the original church – the monastery of Hagios Ioannis Prodromos – was built by the Empress Theodora. The current church doesn't have much to offer, but the ancient crypt, which is dedicated to Saint Methodios, is still there underneath it.'

An old man comes up to us, wrinkled and white-haired, and introduces himself as Alexis. Would we like a tour? I ask him immediately about Methodios, who I can't place at all. He leads us first of all into the crypt, which legend holds to be the basement of the dungeon in which Methodios was kept prisoner.

'Methodios rebelled against the prohibition of images,' Alexis explains, 'and made common cause with the image-loving monks. He was incarcerated for seven years on the orders of Emperor Michael II, the stutterer, who branded the worship of images as idolatry. Michael II was an inhuman man. There are reports that after Methodios was committed to this dungeon, he was punished with seven hundred strokes of the lash. After the Emperor's death, his son and successor Theophilos released Methodios in the year 829 and allowed him to return to Constantinople. In 842 he was elected Patriarch and declared reverence for images as a dogma. But the controversy over image worship flared up again and again, until the iconoclasts were finally defeated under the Empress Theodora II.'

We are by now inside the church and Alexis leads us to the iconostasis, glutted with gold. I wink at Selçuk. Maybe the iconoclasts were sometimes right, after all? We stare at a wall of cloying neo-Byzantine icons. Some of them are so generously loaded with silver that only the enraptured face and slender brown hands are visible amidst the glimmering metal. As we walk outside, the impression remains of a crazy contest between gold and silver. Later it is only the crypt which clings to my thoughts, a small, damp, austere space with a ceiling of whirling tiles arranged in circles, which seems to me, in its thick-necked, peasant way, to represent the cosmos. We thank Alexis and walk through the park, which begins behind the church. Shattered snail shells lie on the path. Weary grasshoppers, disturbed by our steps, once again make their brief upward flight and spread their wings of lilac gauze.

'I have to put this Alexis right,' says Selçuk. 'Methodios isn't the most famous resident of Burgaz; Sait Faik is. That's his house there.'

He points out a slender white wooden house, half hidden by fig and palm trees, with a pergola on the first floor and a roof of bright red tiles. A Greek doctor, one Dr Spanudis, built this villa. The writer, considered to be the father of the modern Turkish short story, lived here for twenty years, from 1934 until his death in 1954. All my friends – Orhan, Sezer, Ferit, Ataol, Ahmet Fıstık as well as Selçuk – love and revere him. There is a photo of him, very well known in Turkey, taken by the wonderful photographer Ara Güler. It shows him on the sun-drenched planks of a sailing boat in Burgaz's harbour.

He's wearing gym shoes and crumpled linen trousers. A black dog with pointed ears is sitting next to him. A straw hat throws his lean, chiselled face into a half-shadow, from which his forehead and nose emerge. His eyes are screwed up and he's holding a pair of sunglasses in his left hand. He looks like the kind of man you'd love to get to know.

In front of his house, he is once more sitting on the steps, in dusky bronze, somehow turned out too small. It reminds me of Fernando Pessoa, of the sculpture in front of his favourite café in Lisbon: the proportions aren't quite right there either. Perhaps it is not permitted to cast important poets in bronze and to make us feel we are close to the life. They can only be small, black, frozen gnomes, betraying nothing of the breadth of their world of thought.

We ring the doorbell. An old woman opens the door. Selçuk unleashes a torrent of Turkish words upon her. I understand nothing except that now, at midday, is not a visiting time, but in the end she unwillingly lets us come in. The house is a museum, but you don't notice it's a museum. It is a Turkish home with furniture, *kilimler*, tables and chairs, quantities of knick-knacks and the writer's writing table. Next to the brass bed stands a wicker sofa and a bathroom cabinet with mirror. On the walls are some photos and a portrait of Sait Faik, painted by Bedri Rahmi Eyuboğlu in vigorous colours of dark blue and green. The poet sits on a throne surrounded by plants and stylised mermaids. Autumn light streams through the tulle curtains. From the pergola the view looks out over the little park. The fat dome of the church rises up over the unkempt green; behind it lie the sea and the tip of Heybeliada.

For me this church and this house, in their contradictory ways, rule over this contradictory town. On one side is the assertion of Christian faith, made into stone, built with no feeling for the texture of light in this island world. On the other, the airy, playful house of the poet, immersed in palms, with cats cosying up to it, a house that could as well be the house of René Depestre on Haiti or Derek Walcott on Saint Lucia.

I know only a couple of stories by Sait Faik and his novel *A Barge called Life*. A curious love of the everyday runs through these texts. For the greatest poverty he nevertheless found poetic, lightly ironic images. He always acts as if he is telling the story for himself alone, without any real feeling for period or drama. But these sharply detailed perceptions of the life of fishermen and small shopkeepers in Burgaz, these daydreams, these precise observations and philosophical aphorisms have something seductive about them. The novel takes place on Burgazada and concerns a young Turkish woman, Melek, who becomes an apprentice in the hairdressers of the Greek Dimitro. I would like to quote from one place in the book, a brief, sardonic passage about beach life on Burgaz in the 1930s, as perceived by Fahri, Melek's friend:

'Many wealthy young men, the sons of Greek businessmen, were behaving as if they were men of the world on a European beach; they were aping the movies. There was endless dancing. The young girls thought: 'I will find the man of my life on the beach'; the young men said: 'You can seduce a girl on the beach.' The young people thought of nothing else; they erupted into resounding, artificial laughter; when they danced, they put on a show in a thousand ways. For the sake of the show even some young Jewish men laughed at the meaningless babble and behaved so as to demonstrate that they were in good spirits; they laughed at the most everyday things, where there was nothing to laugh at, with their hands planted on their hips. And among them there was a type of 'Levantine', oh my God ... as if they were colonial masters. For them all the rest were natives.'

It is difficult to project this scene onto the almost deserted seafront where we are walking: one woman with several bags on a bicycle; two fishermen with white moustaches on white plastic chairs; a young boy next to them, mending a cast net and talking with the old men. I don't understand their Turkish. Yet again I'm glad that Selçuk's English is so good. Granted that he knows only five or six hundred words. But that includes some fancy ones and perhaps we don't even need that many, because we are slowly becoming friends with each other and you can speak in any number of ways and words will be of no use to you, if spirit or friendship is lacking. When Selçuk talks about things he loves, about a flower or a painting or about Orhan Veli Kanık, even in English, he works himself into a kind of beautiful frenzy, so that I always end up asking myself why I am not wearing such a flower behind my ear or why I still haven't learnt one of Orhan Veli's poems by heart.

Following the great arc of the coast road, we have left the village, the mosque and a prayer room for Alevites at the edge of town behind us. In front of us looms an elongated, imposing building of heavy stone blocks.

'The dormitories of the monastery of Saint George,' remarks Selçuk.

'Saint George again!' I blurt out.

Past the building a path leads to a raised cloister with a free-standing bell tower, with three bells hanging in it. The cloister is enclosed on the side facing the hill by the façade of the church. It's almost the same scene: an old, stooped man comes out of the dormitory and shuffles up to us. His hair is knotted into a white pigtail, his face breaks into a thousand creases: *Kalimera!*

He unlocks the church door. The interior is small and very well cared for. The smell of incense envelops us. The iconostasis, here covered in gold, must have been brought to the newer church from the older one, because the old Greek man explains to us that all the icons are from the 18th and 19th centuries. He shows us the inscription on the reverse of one of the icons: 'From Your servant Joachim, a monk from Crete, in the year of Our Lord 1818'. He also tells us that the oldest church on all the islands stands here on the summit of Christus Mountain – '*Hristos Tepesi*', he says. The remains of the monastery of Theokoryphotos are Byzantine, a part of the katholikon dates back to the 9th century, from the time of Emperor Basilius I, with elaborately worked capitals of white marble, very similar to those in Hagia Sophia or the Church of Saints Sergios and Bacchus in İstanbul. Would we be interested in climbing up the mountain? He would send his son along with us. I suddenly feel very hungry however. And Selçuk looks as if he isn't particularly keen on more churches. So we decide to head back to the village.

As the ferry back to Büyükada is to leave in barely twenty minutes, we take a seat in a restaurant next to the *iskele*. At one table sits a man with a snow-white garland of hair, a stack of books next to his glass of wine. It's Arif, the sociologist from the table of regulars at Prinkipo.

'What are you doing here, Arif?'

'I've been visiting a friend, who is working on the reforestation of the island.'

We order baked sardines and Kavaklıdere, the white wine, of which I've already had good experiences and which is quickly

shooting around my bloodstream. Arif is a Green. He wants to preserve the Islands and their woods. A forest fire on Burgazada four
years ago wiped out a great part of the tree population. From a boat
you can see the bald hilltops behind the village. We begin to talk
about the threats to the Islands.

'A law was enacted in 1984,' says Arif, 'designating the Islands as a
nature reserve. For unscrupulous investors in İstanbul, this law was
the signal for the destruction to begin.'

In the long term he is pessimistic. Not on account of the earthquakes – 'these old wooden buildings sway about beautifully' – nor
on account of the islanders, who are sensible people, but on account
of the speculators and politicians. These politicians pursued plans,
which he could only describe as 'Hitler projects'. They have in all seri-
ousness considered building a bridge from the airport in Yeşilköy to
the Islands. The politicians are, every one of them, 'thieves'.

He appends some philosophical reflections to this observation:
'It's the job of rulers to pretend to be monumental. The Byzantine
emperors were already doing the same thing. The Islands were always
the flipside of the imperial city. Here it included nasty little plots
with graceful little gestures and rustic monasteries of solid stone with
plenty of monk's cells, which can easily mutate into dungeons. Generally, however, things stayed peaceful. Indeed, in the 19th and early
20th centuries, the Islands were a paradise, a model of cosmopolitanism. But now megalomania has returned to the government, which
dreams of bridges forty kilometres long and wants to introduce cars
onto the islands.'

The wine is firing him up. Oh yes. Politicians are thieves. Even
the people from the CHP – Atatürk's old Republican People's Party
– have got their claws into the Greek houses on Büyükada and they
don't want to give them up.

Selçuk disagrees. The situation with the old houses is compli-
cated. There are Turkish houses, which speculators have simply let
fall into disrepair. There are Greek houses, for which the owners,
whether they are sat in Athens or in San Francisco, are still paying
the land tax, in order not to lose the land.

'That may be so,' interjects Arif, but the love for the old things,
for what makes up the soul of the Islands, is lacking. He fears that
the character of the Islands, their 'cachet', will be lost. In point of
fact, it has already disappeared: 'Their essential feature was cosmopolitanism. Perhaps there is something like it again today, but it does

not have the same quality. Twenty-three Greeks currently live on Büyükada. Before 1964, there were eighteen thousand. Think about it! Twenty-three Greeks and a handful of Armenians and Jews!'

By now we are sitting on the ferry heading to Büyük, but Arif's anxieties know no limits.

'Even the *faytons* are not what they used to be. They were more beautiful, better cared for, and the horses were groomed night and day.'

We arrive. A *fayton* awaits us, with immaculate corn-yellow basketwork, green upholstery with red buttons. The horses' backs are shining. Selçuk buys a couple of almond rings and gives them to Arif by way of consolation.

'It's not quite that bad,' he says.

It strikes me – as it will strike me again and again – that Selçuk has mastered the art of empathy. It must have deep roots within him.

Later in my hotel I read Orhan Veli in English translation. He really is a damned good poet. The abandonment of traditional forms, the experimentation with free verse, the play on words as words – all European poetry of the last century caught on to these things. But there were some poets who employed these techniques dazzlingly, with perfected artistry, and there were others who used them to give expression to their existential needs. There were, so to speak, jewellers and desperados. Apollinaire was a jeweller, as was Stefan George. Orhan Veli was a desperado.

Crystal chandelier on a wooden cart

THREE YEARS AGO, when some negotiation or other was progressing well in Brussels and EU-accession seemed deceptively close, I was in İstanbul for a short visit.

'We are Ottomans no longer,' screamed Sezer. 'We are Europeans.'

We were sitting in a café on İstiklal Caddesi, one of those fashionable cafés where the customers are the goods on display in the window. The canyon of the street was overflowing; the İstanbulus hurtled past us. Back then I was already dreaming my old dream: a couple of weeks living on Büyükada, fish and rakı, writing. Now I am drinking rakı, I am on Büyükada, I am eating fish, and I'm writing.

But it's curious. Now that I have the cheerfulness, the quiet and the beauty of the Island, my big-city side has roused itself. Suddenly, surrounded by the cries of seagulls, on a sunny square with snoozing dogs in its centre, in the glorious empty café above the ferry building, the desire for İstanbul seizes me. So strongly, that I take the first available ferry. It carries me to Bostancı, on the Asian coast. There is an *iskele* there, built at exactly the same time as the one on Büyükada, with the same architectural ground plan and Arabic inscriptions, only somewhat smaller, not quite so splendid. On the water around the pier is the usual hurly-burly: small launches, barges, some yachts. I run to the next pier to catch the sea bus to Kabataş. These express ferries are like jumbo jets, with none of the charm of the old, eccentric, yet opulent *vapurs*.

There is no open upper deck, only a vast glazed, enclosed space with long, narrow rows of seats, which today are completely occupied. In barely fifteen minutes I am on the European side of İstanbul, beneath Taksim Square. I telephone Ferit, Sezer and Ara Güler.

Miraculously, they all have time. I will meet Ferit for lunch, Sezer for coffee and Ara in a bar in Galatasaray in the early evening.

I take a taxi to Tünel, the beginning of İstiklal Caddesi. This is the heart of the old Beyoğlu district, here are the antique shops and cafés, as well as a number of newly revamped restaurants, although in the side alleys there are still the dubious *gazinos* and bleak tea houses from a bygone age, with the ever-present Father of the Turks on the wall. Having still a little time, I allow myself to drift. I'm really not used to having so many people around me. A young shoeshine boy pursues me. In the end I give in and let him clean my shoes. It's a comfortable feeling, like when the hairdresser massages your scalp. Here it is the surface of the feet, the foot scalp. Everything proceeds like a ritual, which I at first endure, then enjoy. Brushes, application of colour, application of grease (coupled with a delicious sensation), brushes again, then polishing, cross-ways, with a soft cloth. A quick rap on the sole of my foot is the sign that I need to switch feet. I obey. A good introduction. I am becoming a part of the street, the maelstrom. I am adapting my legs, my weight, my posture, my gaze for the city.

Of all the cities I know, İstanbul is the richest in memories and the most forgetful. You can learn a great deal here about the practice of forgetting and remembering. I don't only mean the ancient world and its steady disintegration, nor Byzantium, the new Rome, crumbling to dust on the other side of the Golden Horn. I feel it almost more strongly here on the Pera side, in this 'young' area, Beyoğlu, the cosmopolitan, polyglot heart of İstanbul in the 1930s and 1940s. With the Greek and Arabic and French inscriptions on the doors of its houses, with its caryatids held up by rot, with its sense of decline from its former greatness, Beyoğlu is my favourite part of the city. Here stands Pera Palas, here live the friends, every one of them Byzantine still, here is the patisserie Markiz with its large glazed tiles from the days of Art Nouveau, here are the bookshops Simurg and Pandora, here are the banks that have little by little built up large art galleries, here are people debating and eating and drinking as if their lives depended on it.

Ferit and I visit an art gallery, which is showing some young Turkish photographers. A photograph by Servet Koçiğit speaks particularly to me. At first sight it seems to the viewer like one of those İstanbul street scenes, which has been photographed ad nauseam. A scrawny, shabbily dressed man is pushing a wooden cart along a street littered with potholes. In the background are the façades of what were once beautiful, and are now terribly run-down blocks of flats in Beyoğlu. Only at the second glance do you notice what is being transported on this cart: a large, magnificent chandelier in the Paşa style. It sparkles, shines, and radiates light, fed by some secret current, an invisible battery. For me this surrealist element is a metaphor for longing tied to İstanbul. It certainly alludes to the currently very much in fashion Neo-Ottomanism, an attempt to compensate for the lost significance of the sometime city of the Sultans. The picture also suggests that this city built on two continents presents itself to the visitor as a universe of parallel times and cultures.

Ferit refuses to share my enthusiasm. I half suspect that for him photography is still a second-rank art form, but he doesn't want to admit it.

'You know,' I say, 'that this chandelier stands for the glittering history of your city. There are other cities with long and glorious histories, Alexandria for example. But in those cities we find that nothing remains of this past, they are really only phantom cities. In İstanbul, everything is next to everything else, almost as if the shops, tea houses and financial districts are preserving the Byzantine ruins, as if half a millennium of Ottoman history is turning this city into a booming European metropolis.'

'Is that right?' says Ferit rather morosely. 'The dynamics of today are actually the end result of a whole host of bleak contradictions, tradition versus modernity, western democracy versus Islamic elitism, the massive influx from Anatolia' – at this point he rolls his eyes – 'versus the old, still Ottoman core of society.' He sighs. 'I had hoped that we had advanced a little further. This influx from eastern Turkey has made the gulf between the classes, as well as our big cultural and ethical differences, even worse. You don't notice much of this on your island. Why am I again seeing so many veils and headscarves? Why is it that already, today, the image of an unveiled woman on our streets has become a symbol of Turkey's European identity?'

We continue our conversation in a restaurant.

'You're mourning for the 1970s,' I tell Ferit. 'But the sleepy, lugubrious İstanbul the poets sang about is over. Even the melancholy conjured up by Orhan Pamuk out of the twilight years of the Ottoman Empire, this collective *hüzün*, is no more.'

'And in its place?'

'Chaos and confusion.'

'Do you realise,' asks Ferit, taking his knife in his hand and running its edge along the table cloth, 'that there are people who believe Turkey should be split in two? Draw a line from the mouth of the Bosphorus on the Black Sea, through İzmit and İzmir and finish at Antalya. The smaller part is in their view already Europe, and the larger part can be stuck onto central Asia, Turkmenistan for example.' He laughs. 'These people believe that we would then have done with everything backward-looking, thudding religiosity, illiteracy and any number of other problems. Myself I only know that we need to become part of Europe fast.' He orders himself another glass of red wine. 'All right. Maybe I am a little in mourning for the Levantine and the decadent. But there is a wide-awake secular middle class here, there are superb architects, artists, designers. For the moment there are plenty of spaces of freedom. We must not allow them to be filled in again.'

Ferit is polite and asks about my writing, whether I am making headway with my island book.

'It's moving forward,' I say. 'I'm very happy on Büyükada. The Splendid Hotel, rather weary lady as she is, is perfect for me. And I'm glad that the Islands are my theme. It sometimes happens with journeys that the point of the journey withers and dies. In this case, the opposite has happened. And you can get a grip on the Islands. The expanses of water all around give them grace and beauty. I think I'd have gone mad by now if I were supposed to be writing about İstanbul. There's no more difficult task in literature than capturing a big city in words. How can you get close to İstanbul? That's my question for you. From outside, from Eyüb, which used to be the edge of the city, the large perspective? From within? With your eyes or with your fingers? Is the city best pinned down through its details? The cones of spices in the Egyptian bazaar? The illuminated hoardings at Taksim? The sesame rings? The banks in Levent? The patterns in the black *kilim* from Van? The ubiquitous tulips? The women sitting cross-legged in front of the bakery, their thick, white-skinned soles peeking out from underneath a cheap cloth printed with autumnal roses and lilacs?

'I recommend the following,' says Ferit. 'Go into the Süleymaniya mosque. Since it was forbidden to represent the human form, the great Sinan, like all other Ottoman architects, was entirely focused on the subtle distribution of mass and volume. With simple forms he creates geometries of constant movement. First and foremost, he studied the way the light falls. The 'interior' light should be equally strong at all levels in the space of the mosque, except that on the floor, as you approach the floor, everything flows together, at that point where the forehead is laid down during prayer. If I had to describe İstanbul, I'd begin with that light, on the floor of the mosque.'

Sezer and Ferit are like morning and evening. Sezer is energy, Ferit is contemplation. Sezer is extrovert, Ferit is at peace with himself. Sezer is a dervish, Ferit is an aesthete. Sezer is a dynamo constantly running, recharging its batteries every hour. Friends call her affectionately 'the witch' or 'Paşa'. She is both. And I am saying that very affectionately. I am sitting in her lovingly decorated home in Cihangir. Choice Byzantine and Ottoman objects sit in the windows. On the bright yellow-painted walls hang pictures by the most important Turkish painters, Orhan Peker, Ömer Uluç, Sarkis, Avni Arbaş, Mehmet Gün, cheek by jowl with large format sheets of calligraphy. A fluffy, corpulent Persian cat is stretched out on the sofa. It examines me morosely, gives a brief hiss and then closes its eyes. Sezer brings tea and *şeker pare* –a sugary pastry also known as 'Maidens' Breasts'. The confectioner must have injected a kilo of honey into these small, bulging hillocks of dough. Onto the peak of each bulge he has pressed a small, dark pink almond.

'For you, for the Islander,' she says in a voice implying that nothing is available over there except sour olives and old sardines. Sezer graduated from the Austrian gymnasium in İstanbul and has mastered the German language in all its nuances. She has smuggled Thomas Bernhard, Hans Magnus Enzensberger and many other German-language authors into Turkish. At the moment she is writing a biography of Thomas Bernhard.

'Writing, writing,' she shouts. 'My life is slipping by! I want to fall in love and not write! It's so tedious! I want to be drinking with my friends and not sitting in front of a computer! And you, have you found a girlfriend there' – she means on Büyükada – 'in the beach-front villas, in those gloomy boat sheds?'

We laugh. We talk about this and that. She heats up two small blue balls in a frying pan in the kitchen and then paces three times around me, the pan in her hand – the blue pearls fuming like heathen incense – and mumbles a couple of Turkish phrases.

'That'll help. That'll get you a girlfriend on Büyükada!'

I tell her about my conversation with Ferit. She and he are at war just now.

'Huh, Ferit! The capitalist! His eccentricity is actually all a mask. I see it like this: there are three phases in the history of this country. First of all, the obsolete model, the Ottoman Empire. You can, like Zafer Şenocak, like Orhan Pamuk, equate this phase with a 'culture of melancholy': the awareness that something great has come to an end and this greatness can never be revived. But we have left that entirely behind us. Then phase two, which begins with the founding of the Republic in 1923, when Atatürk abandoned İstanbul and established a new capital in Ankara, which was a completely blank page, an Anatolian Hicksville. I describe this phase as a 'culture of agitation'. Our rulers – Atatürk and his successor İsmet İnönü and their followers – announced a radical alignment to the West. The Republican culture under Atatürk struggled against a rather apologetic culture, which wanted to preserve the old values at all costs. Ferit is stuck in this phase. But today things are so permeable, there is exchange by osmosis. Zafer Şenocak named it a 'culture of translation', which I think is very apt. The conflict between Islam and modernity will slowly be resolved, in parallel with a social transformation, which is proceeding at a furious pace. You only have to open your eyes in the new parts of the city, Levent and so on, and you'll understand immediately what I mean. People are absorbing the current themes from the West into their own traditions and turning them on their head. You can see this 'culture of translation' in Orhan Pamuk's novels, in *The White Castle* or *My Name is Red*, in other authors as well, all of them complex products of the melting pot that is Constantinople-İstanbul.' She hits her chest. 'And I am just such a product too, don't you think?'

Sezer may not know herself, but she knows everybody else. Many, many years ago, in my earlier Turkish life, she introduced me to Ara Güler in Ankara. Ara Güler had come to Ankara to photograph the painter Orhan Peker, a genius who drank himself to an early death. We spent a fantastic evening together, at the end of which Ara gave me two photographs, which I guard as great treasures to this day. One is a studio portrait of the painter, with his girlfriend and his cat in his workshop. Orhan Peker has intense, smouldering, jet-black eyes, which sear the viewer.

The other photograph shows an alley lined with wooden houses in Arnavutköy, a hamlet on the Bosphorus, now incorporated into the sprawling city. This alley doesn't exist any more. The threat of fire hangs over the city every day. It has often burned 'from one sea to the other', from the Horn to the Sea of Marmara. Old Stamboul consisted almost entirely of wooden houses like those in this photograph. It must have been like a forest consumed by fire. This alley, bathed in a dazzling yet gentle morning light, exists now only in this photograph from 1957. Ara Güler is surely the most famous photographer in the country. His photos of İstanbul date back to this period – the 1950s –: the outlines of the minarets cloaked in the black smoke of steamers, the Galata Bridge in the snow, trams in Beyoğlu, fishermen and stevedores on the banks of the Golden Horn, a poorly lit ferry sailing from Eminönü. He captured as no one else has the *hüzün*, the broken glamour of old İstanbul. These pictures have become icons in the history of Turkish photography. I'm pleased to be seeing him again. He owns a house near Galatasaray. He lives there, but he also uses two floors for showing his work and on the top floor he has his studio and his archive.

On the ground floor of the house is a café, which he runs and for which – to his very great annoyance – he has not received an alcohol license. We drink whiskey out of thick, tall porcelain cups. He looks as he looked then, only much older. He is now eighty years old. He has worked for *Time Life*, *Paris Match* and *stern*, he has travelled round the world and has pocketed a thousand honours. Here he sits, a small, miraculous bear with a large, pronounced nose, grey-flecked beard, heavy eyebrows, agile brown eyes and a deep, warm voice. We speak in broken English. I ask him if he has taken photos of the Princes' Islands.

'I really like the Islands,' he says. 'I went as a child and have been back often since, later on in the expectation of catching some faint aroma, some hazy image of that glorious time, when İstanbul was still a true metropolis of many races, religions and sexes. I was not disappointed. But did I take any photos? I pretty much only took photos when I had a commission. I've never had a commission for

Büyükada. I'll have to go up to my archive. Perhaps I'll find something for you!'

Sitting there like that, alert, ironical, with all the cultures stored up inside him, he is for me İstanbul itself, an İstanbul that is slowly disappearing. I sense the warmth of his heart. I sense his understanding of humanity. I invite him to come to Büyükada. The carriages and horses could be a rewarding subject. As could my Splendid, with its austere courtyard and the waiter who has nothing else to do except bring a bottle of rakı in the evening to me, the last remaining guest.

'I'll think about it,' he says and blinks those eyes, eyes which half a million times have given the order to his forefinger to press the shutter release, each time they have found their object. 'Do you still want to have a look over my exhibition spaces?'

A staircase in the rear of the café leads up into Ara's private house. The black-and-white photos of İstanbul, which made him famous, are hung in four rooms on the second floor. Pictures of stevedores and drunks, of a singer in a packed dive in Beyoğlu, of children in the cemetery of Eyüb. There is a dash of social criticism in these photos, but almost completely eclipsed by the intimacy with the subject and the photographer's compassion. Back then, half a century ago, this was surely a new visual language, with echoes in literature as well, such as the multi-layered İstanbul novel *A Mind at Peace* by Ahmet Hamdi Tanpınar, which was published in 1949, at the same time as Ara Güler was beginning to capture his city in calm, dark, almost majestic shots. He smiles with a hint of stoicism and beckons me on to the next storey. Suddenly everything is different: large-format colour photographs, predominantly taken for *Life* and *stern*, of India, South Africa and the USA. Riveting reportage, which nonetheless doesn't reach the poetry of the photos of his home city.

Later we are sitting in his studio. Acting on a sudden inspiration, he yanks an old photo album out from underneath boxes and tins.

'My mother put this together,' he says.

He browses through the album. The translucent tissue paper with a spider pattern on it rustles between the card pages. Then he finds the page he is looking for, a pair of slightly browned snapshots of people in modest swimming costumes in front of an old-fashioned wood cabin.

'That's Yörük Ali Sahili. In those days it was the most popular beach for swimming on Büyükada. And this is me.' He indicates a little whipper-snapper between two hefty women. 'My mother and my aunt.'

Other photos show pretty water nymphs on a wooden jetty.

'I think I already had a sense, I must have been six years old, a feeling for the beauty of the White Russians and for the pleasure of water under the midday sun.'

'Come to Büyükada,' I urge him as we say goodbye.

He puts his arm on my back and leads me down and out of the building. I turn around again and wave. Now I see the logo over the entrance to the café. It's called ARA.

The point and the flat

MACIDE'S PALE BROWN LEGS remind me of the prayer candles in the monastery of Saint George. They look ready to burn. I'm a little concerned, as the sun rises ever higher above the horizon into the sky. Selçuk is sitting in the bow, wiping his forehead. Then a round black cloud glides into the centre of my vision, and Karayan, the fisherman, seems perturbed.

'Let's hope the wind doesn't change,' he says. 'We could have a storm in a second.'

But the black cloud discharges its load to the west of Heybeli, and a vast rainbow appears on the horizon. Macide's legs stay dry, with their tiny blonde hairs. It's as if she has become part of the boat. She plunges a hand into the water. She watches the sky, clear again. I watch her. Behind the hills on Burgazada the sky is almost white. An hour ago it was still reddish. And I thought to myself, Macide knows these hyacinth reds, from her sleepless nights.

I've been looking forward to this excursion for days. Karayan, fisherman and Macide's father, promised me in Ahmet Fıstık's bar that – 'on a suitable day' – we would go to Sivri and Yassı Ada, the two small islands which lie in the Sea of Marmara rather separate from the rest of the archipelago and further from the Asian coast.

'Their shores are full of fish,' he said. 'We used to catch great quantities of fish and prawns in our nets. We'll spend the night on Sivri. There's a small sheltered bay.'

This morning at seven o'clock we met – Karayan, Macide, Selçuk and I – at the fishermen's quay on Büyükada. The weather forecast predicted an unusually warm day for this time of year. Karayan hoisted the sail at first, but the wind was very weak. He fired up the motor and we chugged westwards past Heybeli and used the hill on Burgaz to plot a course across the open sea towards Yassı.

Yassı, or Plati in Greek – both words mean, roughly, 'flat' – appears in front of us like a large cake made of rock. I have gathered from a guidebook that the island is a mere three hundred metres long by one hundred and ninety metres wide. In between the recent buildings on this flat stony expanse, two towers and a crenellated wall rise up, silhouetted against the light. This is what remains of a castle built in 1857 at the behest of a loopy British ambassador to the Sublime Porte, Sir Henry Bulwer, for his beloved Eurydike Aristarchi. He had received the island three years earlier from the Sultan as a gift. Sir Henry was the brother of the great Victorian writer Edward George Bulwer-Lytton and uncle to Edward's son Robert, Viceroy of India. He had barely been accredited in Topkapı when he became involved with the Princess of Samos, this Eurydike. For her he commissioned, on this bleak Island in the middle of the Levant, a vast, grim medieval villa, guarded by towers. The conservative Turkish fishermen tell tales to this day of the indescribable orgies that are supposed to have taken place behind these high walls. Sir Henry Drummond Wolff, a contemporary of Bulwer, described the princess as 'a woman of exceptional charms and wide education, courted by many an ambassador, and an intimate of the Sultan's harem.' Plainly she involved herself in too many intrigues and machinations, as in 1872 she was expelled from the country as a Russian agent. Henry Bulwer sold the island soon after for a horrendous sum to the Khedive of Egypt, İsmail Paşa, who never himself moved into the castle and gradually let it fall into decay. The 1892 edition of *Murray's Handbook* describes the former pleasure palace as a 'dilapidated *Anglo-Saxon Castle*'.

Karayan moors at a little cement pier beneath the more recent buildings. We climb up a staircase to reach the restored entrance gate between the two towers. The picture that greets us behind the crumbling, crenellated wall is desolate. My French informant Gustave Schlumberger, who visited Yassı in 1882, abandons his usual composure and calls the castle 'a bizarre building, a triumph of the worst possible taste and the outgrowth of a diseased imagination'. We have to remind ourselves that our Gustave strolled through these deserted halls only ten years after the Egyptian Viceroy had bought the fortress. The halls appeared to him to be infested by nocturnal birds and bats.

'It offers,' he writes, 'an image of the most grievous neglect. In the courtyard of the large villa, cluttered with mundane detritus, indescribable chaos, our gay picnic resembled a fantastical meal in front of a Sleeping-Beauty castle built as a stage set. His Egyptian Majesty's caretakers, poor, hungry devils who live by catching fish and tending a tiny vegetable patch on the miserable soil, watched us enviously, waiting for our departure before falling on the remains of our feast and devouring them at their leisure in the 'library', with its dusty, empty shelves, a room a little less devastated than the rest, which they have chosen as their home.'

Macide has no interest in white-painted, peeling ruins exuding melancholy. She stays near the pier and looks into the clear water, on the hunt for fish and sea urchins. Selçuk remarks that I have no use for the modern, unadorned buildings, which have been inserted into the puzzling remains of the castle.

'They're from 1960,' he explains. 'They were built for the trial of Adnan Menderes, the Turkish Prime Minister. The army had deposed him. He was a puppet of the Americans and a criminal. After a lengthy trial here in this building – the other one was a comfortable prison – he and two of his ministers were sentenced to death. The three were hanged, not here, on another island, İmralı Ada in the south west of the Sea of Marmara.'

Selçuk and I walk around the island. Of a Byzantine monastery, erected in the 9th century and mentioned as late as 1943 by Ernest Mamboury in his guidebook, there is nothing to be seen. Nothing except rocks, lowly Scots Pines, and Judas Trees.

'They blossom in May,' says Selçuk. 'The whole island is awash with bright violet blooms.'

As we walk back to the pier I think about what a crazy history even the smallest of the Islands has. The monastery of Saint Ignatius, erased by time, a decrepit, entirely out-of-place castle complex from the late Ottoman period, and some equally deserted modern buildings, in which the history of the Turkish Republic was written.

Karayan, having set his nets, calls out: 'Let's get on to Sivri', as if that were the real destination of our trip.

We resume our old places in the boat, Selçuk at the bow, Karayan at the stern holding the tiller, Macide on the bench. We sit facing each other. A vein runs round her ankle like a slender bracelet. We smile at each other. She doesn't seem shy, just a little awkward. From her father I know that she is seventeen years old and attends the secondary school on Büyükada. How many years of English has she done? Our conversation is halting, odd words back and forth. With Karayan and Selçuk she switches into Turkish.

'What does Sivri mean?' I ask.

'"Point"', answers Selçuk, 'or "pointed". In Greek, Oxia, which means the same thing.'

I read in a guidebook that even this fragment of an island had a monastery. Plainly nothing could scare the monks away, because this 'Pointed' consists really of little more than a single steeply sloping reef of rock. The katholikon of the Archangel Michael is already mentioned in a catalogue of 1158, commissioned by the Emperor Manuel I Comnenus. A later traveller, Petrus Gyllius, mentions a visit to the monastery in 1545.

'But this Island's sad claim to fame,' as Selçuk puts it, 'is much more recent. On a number of occasions all the feral dogs roaming around İstanbul were collected together and abandoned on the island. The last time was in 1911. The animals tore each other apart. A horrible massacre.'

Macide shudders. The slender vein on her ankle has withdrawn into her foot.

We sail into a small bay. There are still remains of the harbour, which probably belonged to the monastery, and remains of old walls. The sun is now almost directly above us. Clouds shaped like camels rush through the sky overhead. We decide to have a little picnic first on the harbour mole. I have brought bread and sheep's cheese. Karayan unwraps some green olives from sheets of newspaper and pulls out a bottle of Yakut from underneath some ropes. He tells us that he came here often last autumn and fished for days on end. Sometimes he felt as if he could hear the distant, inhabited islands falling silent, the summer visitors departing one by one, and the natives unburdening themselves and withdrawing irritably into their little cafés and tea houses. Sometimes it was even as if the last voices and laughter before the winter reached him over the surface of the sea like a whisper, just as the quiet now reaches over the water to us.

It is truly very quiet in all directions. One time we hear a boat engine, another time the sounds of a rowing boat, which appears for a moment and then disappears again behind the rocks.

'They're fishing for swordfish,' remarks Karayan.

Then the sound of water, close and loud. Macide has taken off her skirt and T-shirt and has jumped off the mole into the sea in a black swimsuit. She walks along the rocks with a trident and a basket. Then she dives, dives again and resurfaces, her hair over her diving goggles, and carefully places a sea urchin into her basket, her face beaming. An image comes into my head from an earlier summer in a fishing village near Bodrum. I was there with Ferit. He collected several dozen beautiful, plump sea urchins, gleaming in the sun and moving their black spines. Ferit sat down on a stone, with his bucket of sea urchins next to him, and opened the animals with a pair of scissors, pushing the point of the scissors into the body and then slowly cutting them into two. He removed the waste from the shell leaving only the delicious orange strips. We ate these reddish stars with ice-cold Lal, a Turkish rosé, a terrific match for the salt, the seawater and these delicate creations.

Macide returns with a basket full of these black, glistening animals.

'For our supper!' she cries proudly.

Karayan wants to row the boat out and cast his nets for the bigger fish. Selçuk stays on the harbour, guarding our provisions and reading. Karayan rows. Macide now sits on the point of the boat's bow. I crouch directly on the floor. I cannot see the water, only how the bright blue transparent arch of the sky glides over me like a river.

Then I sit up. The sea is perfectly still. Macide has put a towel over her powerful shoulders. Her face is elegantly proportioned. All its parts, the forehead, nose, eyes and mouth are large, but they harmonise wonderfully together and convey an intensity rooted in her thick, arched eyebrows and dark-brown eyes. She has something of the village girl about her, but with a bold charm of which she is entirely aware.

'Why is your father rowing like that?'

'He's making use of the currents.'

Then Karayan pulls the oars in and throws the anchor into the water. The boat loses speed, jolts a little, and then stops. Karayan pulls a large sieve through the water. Unbelievably, just a few pulls are enough to reward him with several langoustines.

'Macide, I can hear something.'

We look up and a school of dolphins glide past, leaping arcs.

'So elegant,' says Karayan and at the same moment I am thinking that these gleaming silvery animals are the most stylish creatures on earth.

'Why are they so elegant?' I ask Macide.

'Because they don't have to move on the hard earth like us, but instead emerge from the soft water and dive back into the soft water.'

The sun is lower in the sky, the seagulls are screeching and crying in a frenzy, cormorants emerge from the water and madly beat their sodden wings to gain speed. But the sea is still calm, except for the waves some distance away striking the black rocks of Sivri.

Karayan carries on catching langoustines. Green fringes of algae flutter in his sieve. I leap quickly out of the boat and swim, the cool water on my ribs and on my back. Macide has caught three bream.

'That'll be enough,' says Karayan.

We row back to Sivri and pull the boat out onto the shingle beach. Macide and Selçuk hunt for firewood for our fire. A last violet light dances hopelessly in the little bay. Then it is dark. The little lighthouse over on Yassı begins its work, its light flashing every two minutes. We slurp down the sea urchins as a starter. Karayan lays a sheet of metal on the stones encircling the fire, rubs the bream with oil and garlic, stuffs their bellies with fresh fennel and lays them on the hot metal. They sizzle fiercely.

'So what do you think of nights on Sivri?' he asks me.

We sit in a circle around the fire. Once, as I'm reaching for the wine bottle, my knee touches Macide's pale brown leg. The wind makes the sea whisper and grumble. Though it is by now completely dark outside the light from our fire, the seagulls are still crying like fury. I feel the desire to get closer to the others and to the fire. I take a bream and squeeze a lemon over it.

'What's up with you?' asks Karayan again.

'I'm thinking about the dolphins.' I shove a piece of fish into my mouth, with a piece of bread, which I've wiped across the metal sheet. 'They're the poets.'

'What?'

'I think the dolphins are the poets.'

Macide wraps herself up in a blanket next to me and watches us with sleepy eyes. Then she falls asleep on the spot.

We three men carry on eating and drinking. The seagull cries continue.

Selçuk, who is drunk, sighs: 'I've often been in love too. Women? Fame? Wine? Orhan Veli said about this problem: "Glasses turn into bottles."'

The fire dies down to a red glow. The moon rises up from behind the reef. Selçuk has gone to sleep now as well. I'm having difficulty finding sleep. In the distance the last ferry passes by, its navigation lights on the bow and sides. It's so beautiful, I say to myself, but I can't wake the others to show them this ferry. Then I fall into an uneasy sleep, dreaming of the hunger of gulls.

Kamariotissa

MY LAST DAYS on the Princes' Islands have dawned. There are signs of it. Yesterday, when I returned to my hotel, there were two electric heaters standing in my room. The manager with the beautiful name Ömer Hayyam apologised.

'We've turned the heating off. You're the last guest.'

But today the morning is warmer than in recent days. I sit without pullover or scarf on the terrace of my Splendid. It is my last day, and I am in the half sad, half uncertain mood of someone who must say goodbye. There are white and dark clouds over the *iskele*, seagulls around the statue of Atatürk, a gentle quiet, the shimmering green of the gardens. The image of a world filled with peace, music and happy people presses itself upon me, an affectionate world, without ambition or violence. But is it really like that? The islands have become for me a symbol of serenity, of beauty, but also a symbol of loss.

The sickness of Byzantium was followed by the glory and then the sickness of the Ottoman Empire. The Islands had their glory days in the face of that empire's collapse. A combination of laissez-faire, Levantine ostentation and dancing on the volcano. From this unending struggle with ruin arose a decadence, which we sense still, in the foyers of the Splendid, under the painted coffers of the John Paşa Köşkü, on the terraces of the ferry building. Is this what I like about the Islands? The fading elegance, the gentle decline, the shadows of a decadence which is itself no more, but which has fought successfully against all forms of worthiness. The idea that things can only get worse, precisely because they are still so enchanting now? There is already a veil of tedium and normality. That may have something to do with the fact that the Islands are no longer a destination for the rich and beautiful of İstanbul. They fly to Marmaris, Bodrum,

Kos. In winter the Islands are empty. The fat Turk already left four days ago. The morose couple too. The doorman is motionless. Ömer Hayyam sits behind his computer, his face tinged with blue. The last remaining waiter slouches in the doorway to the empty lounge, where once İsmet İnönü, Atatürk's successor, opened a ball, dancing an Argentinean tango with his wife, as Young Turk society in top hat and tails stood in a circle around them. No one expects me to order anything. They know my habits. Rakı and salted nuts in the evening. It's true. I am the last guest, who has fallen for these empty Islands, perhaps because amongst the deserted scenery of yesterday's splendour I can so well imagine the parties, the tittle-tattle about the capital city nearby, the old painters and their models, the poets and their mistresses.

I walk along Çankaya Caddesi once more; I examine each individual villa once more. If European culture is based on the refinement of differences, then the architecture on Büyükada is a paradigmatic example of it. No villa is like any other. The desire of clients and architects to be different from the rest, to surpass the ornamentation of their neighbours, is apparent everywhere. It is a sensuous thing, a beautiful endeavour in a noble contest. It makes me think of Arif's saying that the Islands were the underside of the Imperial city. Yes, it's true that under the Emperors, and then under the Sultans, there were any number of horrific excesses here as well. And yet there were also many modest gestures, quite removed from the oppressive monumentality of the metropolis.

I knock on the door at John Paşa's house. In recent days, at the last minute you might say, Selçuk has tried to arrange a few more excursions, to Kınalı – no I have no desire to go to this island disfigured by huge radio masts –, to Sedef, and to Heybeliada again; even a tour around the gigantic, ghostly, abandoned orphanage.

'But you're a poet,' he keeps on saying. 'You must imagine the hundreds and thousands of Greek orphans who were fed and educated there! What has happened to them? Doesn't that excite your imagination?'

For the time remaining, however, I want to concentrate on Büyükada, on what I already know and what I want to see one more time. Already in the last few days I have picked up Selçuk from his villa to eat lunch with him. That lasted two, three hours. Several times acquaintances and friends showed up and sat down with us. I noticed that I was no longer a newcomer, because I was being integrated into every conversation, even if it was being conducted in Turkish, so easily, so adroitly. Today however really is my farewell tour. Selçuk comes out of the house, locks up and we walk together back to the harbour. I want to go to the Milto-Restaurant again, where Ataol took me on my first evening.

The waiter gives me preferential treatment. We receive an ice bucket for our white wine, while the other guests – there aren't many of them – have nothing. Three young women are sitting at the table opposite. Two of them are wearing headscarfs of metallic green material. The third, bareheaded, is photographing the two giggling covered girls. Five cats are waiting at the door. After a delicious fresh blue bream we move on to the Touring Café on the first floor of the ferry building for a Turkish coffee. The windows with their square panes of multi-coloured glass throw a warm, sensuous, almost Cuban pattern of light on the floor and walls, in orange, red, green, blue, the same glowing colours as I will encounter again on the waffle and ice cream stand in front of the ferry building. Here, in the next alcove, not three young women but three elderly ladies are sitting. I cannot believe my ears. They are speaking Ladino, the language of the Sephardim, who came here at the end of the 15th century from Spain, after Ferdinand and Isabella had given them the choice in 1492 between converting to Christianity or leaving the country. Many of them fled to the young Ottoman Empire, which did precious little to look after them. And when the Ottoman Empire was finally dismantled, the Islands continued to reflect the singular nature of that Empire, one vast jumble of languages, religions and cultures. I know from the older travelogues that you used to hear Greek, Turkish, Armenian and Hebrew in these cafés. To listen to these women now in 2008 electrifies me. So the melting pot is not quite done with yet. Selçuk whispers to me that one of the women, a Sephardi Jew, was a famous actress in İstanbul in the 1950s and 1960s. She retired completely to Burgaz thirty years ago and is presumably visiting her friends. So is there more here than the synagogue, more than the old inscriptions on houses and monasteries, bearing witness to the legacy of the displaced? Selçuk runs his finger along his nose and shakes his head.

'Everything is dying out,' he says. 'In the synagogue it's becoming grotesque. At every Jewish ceremony a prayer is read out for the

Turkish president. Red Turkish flags flutter on the roofs of the monasteries. Is that assimilation, or coercion?'

Once again, here in the Touring Café, I come to realise that though the geographical extent of the Islands is very limited, in time you can travel effortlessly back and forth through two millennia.

I walk back to the Splendid. I ask Selçuk to come to Ahmet Fıstık's bar this evening. There's going to be a big farewell feast. In my hotel, beautifully suffused with light, I put in order all the things I have collected, books, maps, the clay figure of Sultan Mihrişah, a perfectly round, reddish stone which Macide gave me during our night on Sivri. It will not all fit in my little suitcase. Most important are the notebooks. So much remains unmentioned, first of all those things I didn't see. My greatest regret is not having visited the only perfectly intact Byzantine church on the Islands, the church of the Blessed Virgin Kamariotissa. This, so I read, is the only chapel in the whole İstanbul area that has retained the tetrakonchos, the clover-leaf layout, unmodified. Around the central dome are gathered four half-domes over exedras, three of which jut out into the outside, while the fourth merges with the narthex. Built in 1439, it must qualify as the last Byzantine church, erected in the vicinity of the imperial city shortly before the Turks captured Constantinople. This chapel stands in the grounds of the Marine Academy on Heybeli and is not readily accessible. You require permission from the commandant of the Academy. I was too lazy to obtain such a thing for myself.

'I'm coming back,' wrote Montaigne in his diary, 'that is my way.'

If I do sometime return to the *adalar*, then it will be first of all on account of Kamariotissa.

The evening is going to become a long one, as always at Ahmet Fıstık's. After a short siesta I sit myself down on the balcony, facing the harbour, and watch the darkening sky over the *iskele*. When the lights in the town come on, I set off for the bar.

The table is actually sagging. Among the vine branches are olives, rakı, wine, sheep's cheese, *tarama*, rakı, smoked sturgeon, aubergine puree, *hummus*, wine, water, lamb cutlets, baked sardines, rakı – and plates and glasses and knives and forks. And above the smeared glasses, lips, cheeks, mouths, words and talk. I hear the clinking of glasses, the melodic Turkish, I see the sparkling eyes and lips and embraces. Ahmet Fıstık embraces me and assigns me my place. He is running the kitchen and staging the banquet at the same time. Furiously rapid, jazzy clarinet music is coming out of the radio.

'Your favourite,' says Ahmet. 'Hüsnü Şenlendirici.'

Hüsnü is a Romany, a crazy clarinettist, known for his outlandish earrings. I heard him once in a club in İstanbul, and have been under his spell ever since.

'The good old days.' Everyone in this drinking hole is talking about them.

I'm the only person talking about the good new days, it seems to me. After my second glass of rakı I wonder, seriously and audibly, whether I shouldn't buy myself one of these ravaged, weather gnawed, debauched wooden buildings, one of these wooden buildings with the colours flaking off them, with crooked balconies, warped window frames, blind windowpanes and spend the days that remain to me here. With Selçuk. With Dima.

Kirkor encourages me.

Selçuk shouts: 'Don't forget the Trotsky house. It's available!'

Ömer joins in the chorus.

It's the light, the ever-present water, the cheerful ships, the warm-hearted islanders, the green-green-green pine forests, the playful cats, the Dolci patisserie, always ready to indulge me.

'Enough reasons?' I ask the group.

'Don't forget the prawns from Sivri!' shouts Karayan.

As if conjured by this word, the waiter brings out baked golden brown fish with salad, lemons and oil. We do ourselves proud. The inebriation deepens. Selçuk stands up swaying, raises his left hand, contemplates it and recites once again the poem on the left hand:

I got drunk and again
I thought of you ...

'Verses by the deathless Orhan Veli!' he says.

I miss Ataol, who has had to travel to Berlin with Anna Karenina for a conference. Only Füsun is taciturn.

'Are you writing poetry?' Özmat, the professor, teases her.

'When you have bought your house,' says Ömer, 'then finally you'll buy *kilimler* from my shop!'

'I definitely will.'

Ahmet Fıstık proposes a game. Together we have to compile a list of the pleasures on Büyükada in the year 1926.

'A gramophone record of Argentinean tango,' whispers Füsun.

'A Maiden's Tower with barometer,' thinks Orhan.

'Karayan's fishing boat as Venetian gondola!' snorts Kirkor.

'And a belly-dancer, but modestly dressed! Things were strict in the early years of the Republic!'

Ömer throws in a wicker chair, 'from the Prag-Rudniker wicker factory in Vienna'. That was all the rage in İstanbul interior decoration back then.

Kirkor: 'Atatürk wearing a white dinner jacket in a snow dome!'

Ahmet Fıstık calls across the table: 'And éclairs from the Markiz patisserie!'

'Penis bien mou,' – a limp dick – is Genghis-Khan-Özmat's comment.

Peals of laughter.

And then Özmat quotes Baudelaire:

Étonnants voyageurs!
Montrez-nous les écrins de vos riches mémoires.

'What does that mean?' shouts Kirkor.

But we're not really getting anywhere.

Ahmet Fıstık roots around on a shelf and returns with three books under his arm: 'My books. Parting gifts for you!'

He begins to sign them and writes on the title page of the first book: 'With affection, for Mrs Sartorius. From Ahmet Fıstık, Prinkipo'.

Özmat, who is leaning over us and keeping a close eye on the ceremony, teases him: 'Mrs! Mrs!'

'That's the vaginafication of my brain,' replies Ahmet, quick as a flash. He crosses through the 's' twice.

The first book is his researches into his childhood on Büyükada. The second deals with the Greeks who have left the Islands and İstanbul but are not happy in Greece. The third is a cookbook with his recipes for the best *mezeler* and 'authentic' fish preparation. All, alas, in Turkish.

'You have to cook those recipes,' everyone shouts. 'Then you'll feel homesick for us.'

Our glasses are filled once more. Ahmet Fıstık raises his glass and looks at me. Then he fires off his final toast: 'May the worst of our days be like these!'

Acknowledgements

To all the friends who have helped me with tips and advice, a big thank you. Leading the way, Sezer Duru, who first showed me the Princes' Islands. Warm thanks also to Orhan Pamuk, Ferit Edgü, Ataol Behramoğlu, Ahmet Fıstık, Ara Güler, Aras Ören and Sabine Vogel. Finally I would like to express my gratitude to Ömer Hayyam, manager of the Splendid Hotel, who gave me the most beautiful room and lent me a quilted jacket when it grew cold.

October 2008–March 2009
Büyükada and Berlin

Bibliography

Deleon, Jak: *Büyükada. A Guide to the Monuments,* İstanbul 2003

Finkel, Andrew: *Postcards from Paradise,* London 1998

Freely, John: *The Princes' Isles: A Guide,* İstanbul 2005

Lilie, Ralph-Johannes: *Byzanz. Das Zweite Rom,* Berlin 2003

Mamboury, Ernest: *Les Îles des Princes,* Ankara 1943

Millas, Akylas: *The Princes Islands. A Retrospective Journey,* Alimos 2002

Pamuk, Orhan: *Other Colours. Essays and a Story,* translated by Maureen Freely, Faber & Faber, London 2007, particularly 'The Islands' pp 79–83

Schlumberger, Gustave: *Les Îles des Princes,* Paris 1884

Tuglaci, Pars: *İstanbul Adalari I,* İstanbul 1995

Ernst Curtius' letters from İstanbul and Prinkipo are quoted from Heinrich Gelzer: *Ausgewählte kleine Schriften,* Hildesheim 1979

The poems of Orhan Veli Kanık are from the volume *Fremdartig / Garip,* Frankfurt a.M. 1985, in a translation by Yüksel Pazarkaya.

The quotation on page ** and two further, not identified quotations, are from the novel *A Barge Called Life* by Sait Faik, published in German translation by Monika Carbe and Enis Gülegen by dipa-Verlag, Frankfurt a.M. 1991.

Orhan Veli Kanık, *I am Listening to Istanbul,* tr Talat Sait Halman, Corinth Books, New York, 1971

OR – a more extensive selection: Orhan Veli Kanık, *Just for the Hell of It,* tr Talat Sait Halman, Yabancı Dil Yayınları, Istanbul, 1997

JOACHIM SARTORIUS, born in 1946, is a poet, translator and commentator. He grew up in Tunis and spent twenty years in the diplomatic service in New York, İstanbul and Nikosia. Until 2000 he was the Secretary General of the Goethe Institut. He has been Director of the Berliner Festspiele since 2001. He lives and works in Berlin. His selected poems were published in English by Carcanet, "Ice Memory", 2006. His most recent volume of poetry, *Hôtel des Étrangers*, was published in 2008.

First published in Great Britain in 2011 by
Armchair Traveller at the bookHaus Ltd
70 Cadogan Place
London SW1X 9AH
www.thearmchairtraveller.com

The moral right of the author has been asserted

A CIP catalogue record for this book is available from the British Library
ISBN 978-1-907973-00-0

Designed and typeset in Garamond by MacGuru Ltd
info@macguru.org.uk
Printed and bound in China by 1010 Printing International Ltd